Comhairle Contae Fhine Gall

Fingal County Council

Items should be returned on or before the last date shown below. Items
may be renewed by personal application, writing, telephone or by
accessing the online Catalogue Service on Fingal Libraries' website.
To renew give date due, borrower ticket number and PIN number if using
online catalogue. Fines are charged on overdue items and will include
postage incurred in recovery. Damage to, or loss of items will be charged
to the borrower.

Date Due	Date Due	Date Due

the French Kitchen

the French Kitchen

MICHEL ROUX JR

RECIPES FROM THE
MASTER OF FRENCH COOKING

WEIDENFELD & NICOLSON

Contents

the French Kitchen

In a French home, the kitchen is the heart and soul of the house. Everything happens in the kitchen – it is at the centre of family life, the place where everyone cooks, eats and gets together for celebrations, and where friends congregate for a drink and snack. For our family, as for many in France, life has always revolved around food and I find that the tastes and smells of certain dishes evoke powerful memories of my childhood and of different times in my life like nothing else.

Food in France has always been about much more than mere sustenance. More often than not it is part of family history, with favourite recipes handed down through many generations and remembered fondly at the table. Regionality in cooking is paramount and fiercely defended. The classics are loved and equally sacrosanct.

I was brought up in a French household, albeit in England, and my family had that passion for good ingredients that you find only in France. My father reared rabbits, pigeons and chickens for the table and we gathered snails and caught crayfish. In summer we searched for wild strawberries in the hedgerows and in autumn we collected chestnuts in the woods. Fishing, hunting and foraging were the norm and part of everyday life for us, not simply a passing fad or a fashionable term on a restaurant menu.

Our family ate traditional French food, of course, and both my parents were fantastic cooks. However busy my mother and father might have been, we sat down and shared a proper meal together as a family at the table, never in front of the television or as a rushed snack.

Many of the recipes in this book are for the dishes that I've enjoyed for years, both at home with the family and at work. They are classics and, with a few adjustments here and there, they are as popular today as they have always been. In fact, I'm often asked to explain what makes a recipe a classic and I think the simple answer is that it is a dish that has stood the test of time. A classic can be anything from a pan of sautéed potatoes, redolent with garlic and herbs, to the most extravagant fish or meat dishes or beautiful pastries. It doesn't have to be complex or difficult to make – a perfect roast chicken, served with some morel mushrooms and creamy mash potato can be one of the best of all meals. A classic can also be a combination of flavours that works so well that it is used in many different dishes, such as sweet and sour, or tomato and basil – such partnerships are the cornerstones of the classics.

We French take mealtimes seriously. We don't see food as mere fuel but as something to be savoured and enjoyed, and this means that you appreciate what you eat all the more. There is always a structure to a French meal, even if it is just a light lunch or family supper, and the menu will be properly balanced. There will be vegetables and salad, and there is always a beginning and an end to a meal. The food must be served properly, not just tossed on the plate. The starter may only be some salad leaves or a few radishes with butter and sea salt, the main course might even be just a plate of charcuterie, but there will be cornichons, good mustard and of course bread – always bread. Cheese is a must for any meal, and it is the French custom to serve it with a knife and fork. Finally, there may be some fruit or yoghurt – always full-fat – and coffee with a little sweet treat if no dessert. This could be a square or two of good chocolate, a little madeleine or calison d'Aix, or some nougat de Montelimar.

There are great dishes in all cuisines but for me, the cooking of France is the best in the world. Perhaps I am biased but in the French kitchen there is a wonderful respect for food that I admire so much. Cookery is constantly evolving and there will always be fashions and fads. But I believe that every keen cook needs to master the essential techniques and be able to roast a joint or bird on the bone, to braise, pot roast, grill and poach and to make a decent sauce. These are the skills that French classics are built on. I like to refer to the great masters of French cuisine – Escoffier, Carême, Boulestin and others. Yes, they may have been working a hundred years ago or more, but interestingly enough you find that there are few techniques used today that they didn't think of first. All the things we now associate with modern cuisine such as jellies, foams and water baths are not at all innovative but old skills and techniques that have simply been given a makeover.

The best recipes allow the ingredients to sing out so that their flavours can be enjoyed to the full. The skill is to respect the food, prepare it with care and present it attractively so that even the simplest soup or salad becomes an exquisite meal.

Embrace these classic recipes for what they are, for the skills that are needed to cook them, for the love that we have for them and the immense pleasure they give. Here are some of my favourites.

La bonne cuisine est la base du véritable bonheur

Good food is the foundation of genuine happiness
AUGUSTE ESCOFFIER

The word *souper* means to have supper and a good soup can indeed be the main part of a meal in France, especially in the countryside. A French soup will be wholesome with plenty of vegetables, perhaps a little meat and, depending on the part of France, some butter, cream or olive oil. Soups are very regional dishes and there are many different recipes for such classics as onion soup – each claiming to be the ultimate. There are also lighter, more elegant soups such as consommés that are ideal served as a starter for a special meal.

Soupes

Crème Crécy

CREAM OF CARROT SOUP

The addition of rice to this soup makes it wonderfully
creamy and smooth. Bacon fat gives a lovely depth, but
you can use vegetable oil if you prefer and if you'd like
to keep the soup vegetarian, make it with good vegetable
stock (see page 320). There are many stories about
the origins of the name of this soup, but it could be
linked to the famous Battle of Crécy, fought between the
French and the British in 1346. Legend has it that the
battle took place on a field of carrots.

Warm the bacon fat or vegetable oil in a large saucepan. Add the carrots and
onion and cook gently until tender, then stir in the rice and continue to cook
for 2–3 minutes. Pour in the stock and simmer for 20 minutes until the rice
is cooked. Slice the heritage carrots into thin slivers on a mandolin and set
them aside.

Season the soup, then transfer it to a food processor and blitz until smooth.
Tip the soup back into the pan and whisk in the butter just before serving.
Add some carrot slivers to each bowl.

SERVES 6

60g bacon fat or 60ml
    vegetable oil
750g large carrots, peeled
    and finely sliced
1 white onion, peeled and
    finely sliced
50g short-grain rice, such
    as paella rice
2 litres chicken stock
    (see page 320)
1 bunch of heritage carrots
    (mixed colours), peeled
100g unsalted butter, diced
salt
black pepper

Biersupp et petites brochettes à la Suissesse

BEER SOUP AND CHEESE AND HAM KEBABS

A classic recipe from the Alsace region of France, beer soup is also popular in Germany, Holland and Belgium. It is absolutely delicious I promise you, and even non-beer drinkers will be won over. Traditional lager works well, but you can use any beer you particularly enjoy, including fruit-based beers. The little brochettes are a perfect accompaniment to the soup or can be served as a snack or with a salad as a light lunch.

Melt the butter in a saucepan, add the onion and cook until soft. When the onion is just starting to take on a little colour, add the breadcrumbs and the lager. Bring to the boil and cook for 3 minutes, then pour in the stock and continue to simmer for 20 minutes. Season with the sugar, salt and pepper.

Blend the soup in a food processor until smooth, then tip it back into the pan and whisk in the crème fraiche. Sprinkle with a little grated nutmeg before serving with the cheese and ham brochettes.

BROCHETTES

Cut each slice of ham in half and cut the cheese into oblongs measuring about 4cm x 1cm. Wrap a piece of ham around each piece of cheese and thread them on to little bamboo skewers or decorative metal ones.

Spread the flour and breadcrumbs on separate plates and beat the egg in a bowl. Dust each brochette with flour, dip it into the egg and finally coat with breadcrumbs. Half fill a heavy saucepan or deep-fat fryer with oil and heat to 180°C, then cook the brochettes until they are golden and crispy. Drain them on kitchen paper before serving. Always take care when deep-frying food and never leave hot oil unattended.

SERVES 4

1 tbsp unsalted butter
1 onion, peeled and chopped
120g fresh white
    breadcrumbs
330ml good-quality lager
500ml chicken stock
    (see page 320)
2 tsp brown sugar
2 tbsp crème fraiche
freshly grated nutmeg
salt
black pepper

PETITES BROCHETTES À LA
SUISSESSE

8 slices of good-quality air-
    dried ham (not too thin)
200g Gruyère cheese, sliced
    1cm thick
2 tbsp plain flour
2 tbsp breadcrumbs
1 free-range egg
vegetable oil, for deep-
    frying

Crème Vichyssoise

CREAM OF LEEK AND POTATO SOUP

I have seen this soup served hot, which is totally
wrong. It should be ice cold, with little embellishment.
However, I must say that the addition of little floating
islands of crème fraiche dotted with chives does make
this great soup into something extraordinary.

Wash and trim the leeks, discarding the tough parts of the dark green leaves,
and slice them thinly. Melt the butter in a large saucepan, add the leeks and
onions and cook gently until translucent and tender. Add the potatoes, water
and stock, then simmer for 20 minutes. Pour in the cream and cook for a
further 5 minutes.

Season the soup, then tip it into a food processor and blend until smooth.
Pass it through a fine sieve into a bowl set on ice and leave to chill. To serve,
sprinkle with chopped chives and some chive flowers, if available, and
drizzle on a little extra cream, if you like.

For the crème fraiche islands, stir some chopped chives into the crème
fraiche, then add small spoonfuls to the soup just before serving.

SERVES 8

700g leeks
50g unsalted butter
300g white onions, peeled
  and chopped
300g potatoes, peeled and
  chopped
700ml water
700ml chicken stock
  (see page 320)
300ml double cream, plus
  extra for serving
1 bunch of chives, chopped
  (with flowers if possible)
crème fraiche (optional)
salt
black pepper

Soupe à l'oignon Lyonnaise

LYONNAISE ONION SOUP

Filling, warming and totally satisfying, this is one of the most famous of all French soups and a true classic. It's made all over the country and almost every region has its own version.

Melt the 60 grams of butter with the tablespoon of oil in a pan over a medium heat, then add the sliced onions. Cook, stirring occasionally, until the onions caramelise and become sweet and tender – don't cover the pan. Once the onions are ready, add the white wine and cook until the liquid has reduced by half.

Melt the tablespoon of butter in a large saucepan, add the flour and mix well to make a roux. Cook until the roux is light brown but don't let it burn. Pour in the beef stock, whisking well, and simmer for 5 minutes. Add the onion mixture, season generously and cook for another 30 minutes. Meanwhile, toast some slices of baguette.

Preheat the grill. Mix the egg yolks, port and crème fraiche together and divide the mixture between heatproof soup bowls. Pour some hot soup to each bowl, stirring it into the egg mixture with a fork. Add some slices of toasted baguette, sprinkle with grated Gruyère and glaze under the hot grill until the cheese is golden and bubbling. Serve immediately.

SERVES 8–10

60g unsalted butter,
   plus 1 tbsp
1 tbsp vegetable oil
1kg best-quality onions,
   peeled and sliced
1 bottle of dry white wine
60g plain flour
1.8 litres beef stock
   (see page 323)
1 baguette, sliced
5 free-range egg yolks
100ml port
250g crème fraiche
300g Gruyère cheese, grated
salt
black pepper

Potage essaü

PUY LENTIL AND PHEASANT SOUP

The French love soups or *potages* and each region, even
each town in some parts, has its own version of the
classics. Puy lentil soup is delicious on its own with
just a drizzle of cream and fried croutons, but to make
it even more special I like to make this soup with game
stock and serve it with little quenelles of pheasant. It's
best to use a cock pheasant, as hens are for roasting and
would be wasted for this recipe. Cock birds tend to be
tougher but cheaper.

Remove the breasts from the pheasant and trim off any skin and sinew.
Place the breasts in a blender with the egg white and blitz until smooth.
Pass the mixture through a fine sieve into a bowl set over ice, then beat in
240ml of the cream. Season with salt, pepper and a grating of nutmeg,
then set aside.

Chop up the legs and carcass of the pheasant. Heat the vegetable oil in a
large pan, add the pheasant bones and fry until they are just starting to
caramelise. Add the onion, carrot, thyme and bay leaves to the pan, cook
for 5 minutes, then cover with 3 litres of cold water and add any bacon
trimmings. Simmer for an hour, then pass the stock through a sieve.

Put the lentils into a clean pan, add 2 litres of the pheasant stock and
simmer until cooked. Remove a few spoonfuls of lentils and set them aside
to use as a garnish, then blitz the rest of the soup with the remaining cream
until smooth. Season with salt and pepper.

Heat the remaining stock in a pan. Shape the pheasant breast mixture into
neat quenelles (egg-shaped spoonfuls), add them to the stock, a few at a
time, and poach for 3 minutes. Grill the bacon slices until crisp.

To serve, place some cooked lentils in each bowl, add a couple of pheasant
quenelles and a slice of crispy bacon, then pour in some hot soup.

SERVES 6

1 cock pheasant
1 free-range egg white
360ml double cream
freshly grated nutmeg
1 tbsp vegetable oil
1 onion, peeled and chopped
1 carrot, peeled and chopped
1 sprig of thyme
2 bay leaves
3 litres water
80g smoked streaky bacon,
    sliced very thin (keep any
    trimmings)
250g puy lentils, washed
salt
black pepper

Soupe à l'ail et aux amandes

WHITE ALMOND AND GARLIC SOUP

This wonderfully summery cold soup comes from the Basque region of southwest France. An essential ingredient is piment d'Espelette, a smoky hot spice made from dried chilli peppers and produced only in this area. The little corn and smoked duck cakes are optional, but they do add extra flavour and texture.

Purée the chopped garlic with the egg yolk in a mini blender or food processor. Start adding the oil, a little at a time, to make a garlic mayonnaise. Scrape this into a bowl.

Put the bread and ground almonds in a food processor, add 800ml of water and blitz thoroughly until really smooth. Tip this into a bowl, then stir in the garlic mayonnaise, vinegar and season. Chill for at least 4 hours.

Serve the soup cold, garnished with a little olive oil and a sprinkling of piment d'Espelette. Add some garlic croutons if you like (see page 339) or serve with some corn and smoked duck cake, which makes a delicious accompaniment to this soup.

CORN AND SMOKED DUCK CAKE

You can use a cake tin for making this or a silicone cake pop mould, which will give you 20 little balls of cake.

Preheat the oven to 200°C/Fan 180°C/Gas 6. Whisk the eggs in a bowl, add the polenta and baking powder, then fold in the rest of the ingredients. Transfer the mixture to your cake tin or mould. If making a large cake, cook it for about 30 minutes or until a skewer comes out clean. If making small balls of cake, cook them for about 10 minutes. Remove from the tin or moulds, cut into small pieces if you've made a large cake, and serve with the soup.

SERVES 6

4 new season garlic cloves, roughly chopped
1 free-range egg yolk
150ml grapeseed oil
3 slices of day-old white bread
250g ground almonds
800ml water
1 tbsp sherry vinegar (or more to taste)
olive oil
ground piment d'Espelette (chilli powder)
salt
white pepper

CORN AND SMOKED DUCK CAKE

6 free-range eggs
200g polenta
1 tsp baking powder
100g smoked duck, diced
160g sweetcorn kernels (canned are fine)
50g tomato paste
90g unsalted butter
100ml double cream
pinch of saffron strands
salt
black pepper

Si un seul élément de la cuisine Française peut être appelé important, fondamental et essentiel, cet élément est la soupe

If any one element of French cooking can be called important, basic and essential, that element is soup

LOUIS DIAT

L'aigo boulido

GARLIC AND SAGE SOUP

L'aigo boulido means 'boiled garlic' and this soup is often prescribed for people who are feeling under the weather or in need of some detox. It is enhanced by a touch of sage, which is also a mild antiseptic and helps the digestion. There are many variations but everyone agrees that this is best made with new season garlic, which is sweet and innocuous.

Peel the garlic and cut each clove into 5 or 6 slices. Put the garlic into a saucepan with the water and some salt, bring to the boil and simmer for 30 minutes. Add the sliced sage leaves and take the pan off the heat.

Tradition has it that you put the stale bread in the bottom of the bowl and pour the piping hot soup on top, with or without a drizzle of olive oil. When you've eaten all but a few spoonfuls of soup, add a dose of wine to your bowl before finishing it off – strictly medicinal of course!

SERVES 4

20 garlic cloves, or more to taste
1 litre water
pinch of coarse sea salt
8 sage leaves, sliced
thick slices of stale country-style bread
2 tbsp strong olive oil (optional)

Velouté de chataignes

CHESTNUT AND APPLE SOUP

A great winter warmer, this soup is a speciality of the Cévennes region of France where chestnut trees grow in abundance. They also make a version in Corsica where they have a thriving chestnut industry. The soup is best made with dried chestnuts, which are sold peeled and ready to reconstitute in water before being cooked.

Soak the chestnuts in water for 3–4 hours until reconstituted, then drain them and rinse. Put the chestnuts in a large saucepan with the thyme, bay leaves, onion and vegetable stock. Roughly chop half the red and half the green apple and add them to the pan. Bring the soup to the boil, then simmer gently for about 40 minutes or until the chestnuts are tender and cooked. Take out some cooked chestnuts to use as a garnish, remove the thyme and bay leaves, then blitz the soup in a blender or food processor until smooth. Season with salt and pepper to taste.

Using a melon baller, scoop out little balls of apple from the remaining halves. Melt the butter in a small pan, add the apple balls and sprinkle them with the sugar. Toss briefly until lightly glazed.

To serve, put a few cooked chestnuts and apple balls in each bowl, pour in some soup, then drizzle with a little olive oil, if you like.

SERVES 4

180g dried chestnuts
1 sprig of thyme
2 bay leaves
1 white onion, peeled and chopped
800ml vegetable stock (see page 320)
1 red apple
1 green apple
1 tbsp unsalted butter
½ tbsp caster sugar
olive oil (optional)
salt
black pepper

Soupe aux abattis

GIBLET SOUP

Tasty, warming and filling, this soup is made with parts
of the chicken that some people would throw away. Not
in France though! We like to use every bit of the bird.

Cut each chicken neck into 3 pieces and the gizzards in half. Trim the
thickest part of each wing to reveal the bone by pushing down the meat so
it resembles a lollipop and keep these for later. Trim the rest of the giblets
as necessary.

Heat a tablespoon of the butter with a little drizzle of oil in a large saucepan
and fry the necks, gizzards, wing tips and combs. Sprinkle in the flour and
stir well until brown, then pour in the stock and 500ml of water. Add the
bouquet garni and seasoning and simmer for an hour or until all the meat
is tender. Pass the soup through a strainer and keep warm.

Pick the meat off the necks and slice the gizzards and combs. Heat a
tablespoon of butter in a small pan and gently cook the sliced celery until
tender. Fry the livers, hearts and wing lollipops in the rest of the butter and
a little oil until golden, then season.

Add the cooked rice to the soup and warm through. Serve the soup in deep
plates with the roughly chopped meat.

SERVES 6

3 chicken necks, skinned
3 chicken gizzards
6 chicken wings, including
   tips
6 cockscombs
6 chicken livers
6 chicken hearts
3 tbsp unsalted butter
olive oil
1 tbsp flour
1 litre chicken stock
   (see page 320)
500ml water
1 bouquet garni, made up of
   thyme, bay leaf, parsley
   stalks and rosemary
   (see page 342)
2 celery sticks, sliced
3 tbsp cooked long-grain rice
salt
black pepper

Soupe de lièvre

HARE SOUP

Even non-game lovers will enjoy this meaty,
wholesome soup. Some versions contain barley, but
I think that the dumplings hit the spot and make this
soup a hearty meal in itself.

Season the hare meat. Heat a tablespoon of oil in a large saucepan and
brown all the meat, except the heart and liver, over a high heat. Add the
carrot, celery, onion, bacon and potato and cook gently for 10 minutes.
Add the bouquet garni and the stock, then simmer very gently for 2 hours –
the soup should barely bubble. Skim the surface regularly and top up with
hot water if necessary.

Take out the hare leg, strip off the meat and dice it. Put this in a bowl with a
little of the soup to keep it warm and moist and set aside. Add the liver and
heart to the pan and simmer the soup for another 20 minutes. Strain the
soup through a fine sieve, then pick off as much meat from the bones as you
can. Purée the meat, heart and liver with a drop of the soup and keep warm.

Bring the soup back to the boil, then whisk in the cold butter, puréed meat
and the port. Serve in bowls with the diced leg meat and dumplings.

DUMPLINGS

Put the flour, suet and seasoning in a bowl and gradually bring them
together with the 2 tablespoons of water. Add the chopped parsley and
knead the dough like bread until it is soft but not sticky.

Leave the dough to rest in the fridge for 20 minutes, then roll it into bite-
sized balls. Bring a pan of salted water to the boil, drop in the dumplings and
cook for 7–8 minutes until swollen.

SERVES 4

2 shoulders, neck and
    ribcage of a hare
1 hare's leg
1 hare's heart and liver
vegetable oil
1 carrot, peeled and chopped
1 celery stick, chopped
1 white onion, peeled and
    chopped
1 x 30g slice of smoked
    bacon, chopped
1 potato, peeled and chopped
1 bouquet garni, made up of
    thyme, bay leaf , parsley
    stalks and rosemary
    (see page 342)
2 litres chicken stock
    (see page 320)
2 tbsp cold unsalted butter
4 tbsp port
salt
black pepper

DUMPLINGS
100g self-raising flour
60g suet
2 tbsp cold water
2 tbsp chopped flatleaf
    parsley
salt
black pepper

Consommé de boeuf à la royale

BEEF CONSOMMÉ WITH ROYAL GARNISH

Gold leaf is the classic garnish for this – the 'royale' touch on top of the little custards served in the consommé. And if you really want to push the boat out you could add a teaspoon of caviar. This is the sheer opulence and decadence of yesteryear – consommé taken to the ultimate level. You'll need little glass serving bowls to set this glorious dish off to perfection.

First prepare the custards for the garnish. Preheat the oven to 120°C/Fan 100°C/Gas ½ and butter 4 small dariole moulds measuring 5 x 5cm. Place the moulds on a baking tray. Mix the egg yolks with the cream and season well with salt, pepper and a grating of nutmeg, then gently pour the mixture into the moulds. Cover with foil and steam the custards for 10 minutes or until they are set. Leave to rest for 10 minutes before taking the custards out of their moulds.

Trim the beef of all fat and sinew and chop the meat as finely as you can. Finely chop the vegetables, then mix them with the egg whites and a generous splash of Madeira. Tip all this into a thick-based saucepan, add the cold stock and place over a high heat. Using a spatula, stir the stock gently until it begins to simmer, then stop stirring and leave to cook slowly until a crust starts to form – this crust lifts all the impurities out of the stock to leave it beautifully clear. Continue to simmer for 20 minutes, then gently strain the stock through a muslin cloth and check for seasoning.

Using a melon baller, make little balls from the courgette, celeriac and carrot. Blanch them briefly in salted, boiling water until al dente, then drain and plunge the balls into iced water.

To serve, delicately place a custard in the base of each glass serving bowl and top with a piece of gold leaf. Add a few of the vegetable 'pearls', then pour in the hot consommé to come halfway up the custard. Serve at once.

SERVES 4

100g lean beef, such as skirt
   or shin
1 small carrot, peeled
1 shallot, peeled
½ white leek, cleaned
1 tomato, peeled
4 button mushrooms, wiped
1 celery stick
½ beetroot, peeled
3 free-range egg whites
splash of Madeira wine
4 litres cold beef stock
   (see page 323)
salt
black pepper

ROYAL GARNISH

unsalted butter, for greasing
3 free-range egg yolks
150ml single cream
freshly grated nutmeg
1 courgette
½ celeriac
1 carrot
4 pieces of edible gold leaf
salt
white pepper

Soupe de moules

MUSSEL SOUP

Mussels are plentiful, cheap, and quick and easy to prepare. The deep-fried breaded mussels I suggest below make a great snack on their own but really do make this simple soup into something special – a meal in itself.

Wash the mussels well and scrub off any beards or barnacles. Heat a tablespoon of the oil in a large pan and gently cook the chopped shallots until soft. Add the mussels, bouquet garni and white wine, put a lid on the pan and place it over a high heat until the mussels have opened and are cooked. Tip them into a colander over a bowl to collect the cooking liquor, then pass the liquor through a fine sieve and keep it for later.

Pick out the mussel meat from the shells and set aside about a quarter of them to make breaded mussels for the garnish.

Add the remaining oil to a clean pan and sweat the carrots, celery, potato and leek until tender. Add the chopped tomatoes and saffron and cook for a further 5 minutes, then add the mussel liquor and fish stock, followed by the mussel meat. Simmer for 10 minutes, then blitz in a food processor until smooth. Pass the soup through a fine sieve and season with salt and pepper.

Now prepare the garnish. Slice the carrot and leek on a mandolin or cut them into fine strips. For the breaded mussels, half fill a large heavy saucepan or a deep-fat fryer with vegetable oil and heat to 180°C. Dredge the mussels in the seasoned flour, then dip them into the beaten egg and coat in breadcrumbs. Deep-fry the breaded mussels in batches until they are crispy and golden.

Serve the soup with fried breaded mussels, strips of leek and carrot and a swirl of crème fraiche.

SERVES 8

6kg mussels
3 tbsp vegetable oil
4 shallots, peeled and
    coarsely chopped
1 bouquet garni, made up of
    thyme, bay leaf and parsley
    stalks (see page 342)
1 bottle of dry white wine
2 carrots, peeled and
    chopped
2 celery sticks, chopped
1 large potato, peeled and
    chopped
1 small leek, cleaned and
    chopped
8 tomatoes, chopped
pinch of saffron strands
3 litres fish stock
    (see page 324)
salt
black pepper

GARNISH
1 carrot, peeled
1 leek, cleaned
vegetable oil
100g flour, seasoned with
    salt and pepper
1 free-range egg, beaten
100g breadcrumbs
crème fraiche

Velouté de coquillages

SHELLFISH SOUP

Velouté means velvety in French and that is the texture
this soup should have. You can adapt the recipe for
different shellfish, according to what is available and
your preferences, but do always include mussels and
clams as they are the base of the soup. Whelks, scallops
and lobster also work really well.

Wash the mussels, cockles and clams in cold water. Trim and clean the
squid, removing the 'beak' and innards from each one – your fishmonger
will do this for you if you prefer. Slice the bodies into rounds and keep the
bunches of tentacles whole. Peel the langoustines and discard their shells.

Put the clams and mussels in separate pans over a high heat, dividing the
wine equally between each pan. Cover and leave to cook for 4–6 minutes,
depending on the size of the shellfish, then drain and keep the juice. Be
careful not to overcook them or they will go chewy. Sear the squid in a very
hot pan for 30 seconds.

Pick out the meat from the clams and mussels and divide this and the rest
of the seafood between the soup bowls. Strain the juice through a fine
sieve into a pan and place it over a high heat. When it boils, add the double
cream and crème fraiche and bring it back to the boil. Season well and add
the lemon juice, then pour the hot soup over the clams and the rest of the
seafood. Grate a little nutmeg on top and serve immediately.

SERVES 6

500g mussels
500g cockles
500g surf clams
6 baby squid
6 cooked langoustines
1 bottle of dry champagne
    or white wine
100g cooked peeled brown
    shrimps
300ml double cream
250g crème fraiche
juice of 2 lemons
freshly grated nutmeg
salt
black pepper

Soupe d'étrilles

BRITTANY VELVET CRAB SOUP

I remember an old Brittany saying that goes something like this: 'When God made sole the devil made skate, and when God made lobster the devil responded with crab'. That's certainly not my opinion. Although the little velvet crabs that live on the coast and in rock pools have little or no meat to be picked, their flavour is intense and sweet – perfect for this classic soup. You can kill the crabs painlessly by putting them into the freezer for an hour; they just go to sleep.

Rinse the crabs in cold water. Heat the oil in a large saucepan, add the onions and cook them until soft. Turn up the heat and add the crabs, stirring them around in the pan until they turn red. Using a rolling pin or meat mallet, crush and break up the crabs in the pan.

Add the saffron, bouquet garni, garlic cloves, half the tomatoes and some seasoning. Pour in enough water to cover everything well and bring it to the boil. Skim any scum off the surface, then simmer the soup for 30 minutes.

Remove the pan from the heat and strain the soup through a metal colander into a large bowl, pressing it carefully to extract all the flavourful juices from the crabs. Then pass it through a fine sieve into a clean saucepan.

Put the potatoes in a pan of water with the seaweed, bring it to the boil and cook until tender. Drain, then peel and dice the potatoes. Cut the remaining tomatoes into small dice.

Warm the soup through in the pan, then stir in the crème fraiche and check the seasoning. Put some diced potato and tomato in each bowl, then pour in the soup and serve with some thin slices of baguette dried in the oven. Alternatively, serve with fried, garlic-rubbed croutons and cheese but a purist would not approve of such frivolity.

SERVES 6

4kg velvet crabs
2 tbsp vegetable oil
4 onions, peeled and sliced
2 pinches of saffron strands
1 bouquet garni, made up of
    thyme, bay leaf, parsley
    stalks, celery and leek
    (see page 342)
4 garlic cloves, crushed
12 ripe tomatoes, peeled
    and deseeded
6 potatoes, washed
    (Charlottes or Rosevals
    are best)
200g seaweed (dulse or
    kombu)
4 tbsp crème fraiche
1 baguette
salt
black pepper

A terrine or a pâté can be a homely, rustic dish – something to have in the fridge ready for everyone to help themselves – or the most sophisticated, elegant creation. Some do take a bit of time and effort but they are satisfying to make, keep well and serve lots of people. These are perfect sharing dishes – something to put on the table and enjoy with friends. A terrine is defined by its long, loaf-like shape and can be made out of almost anything. A pâté, though, is invariably made of meat and is more often than not pork based, as it is the pork fat that gives pâté its richness.

Terrines et pâtés

Marbré d'automne

AUTUMN MARBLED TERRINE

We love making terrines at the restaurant and we've been serving this one since the early nineties. Full of rich flavours, it never disappoints and it's perfectly possible to make at home too. All the ingredients are readily available and it is really impressive. You'll need a terrine dish measuring about 25 x 8cm or you could use a loaf tin. I like to use black trompettes for their colour, but any good wild mushrooms will do. This terrine keeps well in the fridge for about a week.

SERVES 12

1 savoy cabbage
2 boneless, free-range chicken supremes, skinned
3 tbsp duck fat
200ml port
5 gelatine leaves
24 sage leaves
300g wild mushrooms, wiped or washed and any grit removed
2 smoked duck breasts
salt
black pepper

Separate the cabbage leaves, discarding the toughest and any that are damaged. Trim out the stalks and wash the leaves well. Bring a pan of salted water to the boil, add the leaves and cook until tender. Drain, then refresh the leaves in iced water to stop them cooking and drain again. Set aside.

Season the chicken. Heat a tablespoon of the duck fat in a frying pan and sear the chicken on both sides. Add the port, cover the chicken with a piece of greaseproof paper and simmer gently until cooked. Remove the chicken and set aside, keeping the liquid. Soak the gelatine leaves in a dish of cold water to soften. Remove, squeeze out the excess water and add the softened gelatine to the pan with the port. Stir until it has dissolved, then set aside.

Heat another tablespoon of duck fat in a large pan and add the cabbage leaves. Season with salt and pepper, add the sage and cook the cabbage until soft. Pour in the port and gelatine mixture.

Melt the remaining tablespoon of duck fat in a frying pan and sauté the mushrooms until tender. Season and set aside. Remove the skin from the smoked duck breasts and cut them into fine strips.

Line the terrine dish with cling film and place a layer of port-soaked cabbage in the bottom. Now add a layer of mushrooms, more cabbage, then chicken, mushrooms, duck, cabbage and mushrooms. Finish with a layer of cabbage leaves. Wrap the cling film tightly over the top and add a weight on top to press the terrine down. Place the dish in the fridge overnight to set. The next day, use the cling film to help you lift the terrine carefully out of the dish. Slice and eat with toast or garnish beautifully and serve with truffle dressing (see page 233) or herb mayonnaise (see page 333).

Boudin noir

FRENCH BLACK PUDDING

At first glance, this recipe might appear daunting but there is nothing very difficult and the result is so delicious it is well worth the effort. It does make a large amount but the boudin freezes well. A good butcher will be able to supply the pig's head and blood and most Italian delis stock lardo. If using sausage casings, buy the large size. I recommend the crispy pork skin too, which goes perfectly with the boudin.

To cook the lardo, wrap it in foil and bake at the lowest possible setting in your oven for 1½ hours. Leave to cool, then chill and dice. Cut the cooked pig's head and tongues into 1–2cm dice – use everything, the ears, skin, the lot – then mix it all with the diced lardo in a large bowl. Melt the duck fat in a frying pan and gently cook the diced onions until very soft and thoroughly cooked. Add them to the meat and lardo, mix in the pig's blood, spices, 2 teaspoons of salt and the cream, then the herbs, egg whites and vinegar.

You can cook the boudin in terrines or in natural sausage casings. If using terrines, you'll need about 4, each measuring about 23 x 9cm. Grease them well, then spoon in the mixture and cover with greased paper and foil. Place them in a roasting tin, pour in boiling water to come about halfway up the sides, then bake in a cool oven, at 120°C/Fan 100°C/Gas ½ for 2 hours or until set. Leave to cool, then chill until needed. If using casings, roll the mixture into large sausages, about 6cm in diameter. Tie a knot in one end of each casing, fill them and tie securely. Bring a pan of salted water to a gentle simmer and poach the boudins for about an hour.

To serve, slice the boudin, dust with flour and pan-fry in a little olive oil. Serve with spicy tomato chutney (see page 337) and crispy pork skin.

CRISPY PORK SKIN

Make lots of holes all over the skin with a fork, then sprinkle with lots of salt and set aside for an hour. Put the skin in a large pan of water, bring to the boil, then simmer for a couple of hours until the skin is tender and can be pierced easily with a knife. Remove it and when cool enough to handle, lay it between 2 sheets of greaseproof paper on a baking tray. Put another tray on top to keep it flat and bake at 160°C/Fan 140°C/Gas 3 for about 45 minutes until crisp. Break the skin into pieces and store in an airtight container.

SERVES 30

500g cured pork fat (lardo)
1 cooked pig's head (see page 48)
350g cooked pig's tongues (about 4)
50g duck fat
1kg large onions, peeled and diced
750g pig's blood
generous pinch of freshly grated nutmeg
generous pinch of cinnamon
½ tsp ground piment d'Espelette (chilli powder)
2 tsp salt, plus extra for seasoning
200ml double cream
1 tbsp each of chopped tarragon, chervil and flatleaf parsley
2 free-range egg whites
50ml sherry vinegar
500g large pork sausage casings
flour, for dusting
olive oil, for frying

CRISPY PORK SKIN
large piece of pork skin with a couple of millimetres of fat
coarse sea salt

Jambon persillé

HAM TERRINE WITH PARSLEY

As a young chef I worked in a charcuterie in Paris and this was one of my favourite terrines – both to make and to eat. Very French, very easy, this is great for a party and keeps well in the fridge for about ten days.

Cut the gammon into big chunks of about 10cm and place them in a large saucepan of cold water with the trotter. Bring the water to the boil and cook for 3 minutes, then drain and rinse the meat.

Put back the gammon and trotter back into the rinsed pan and add the wine, peppercorns and juniper berries. Tie the parsley, tarragon and thyme together and add them to the pan.

Add enough water to cover the meat. Slowly bring the liquid to a very, very gentle simmer – barely a tremble – and continue to cook the meat for about 1½ hours, until tender. Skim often to remove any scum and excess fat.

Once the gammon is cooked, allow it to cool a little before removing it from the pan and setting it aside to drain. Keep the cooking liquid.

Pass the cooking liquid through a muslin cloth. You should have about 400ml but if there is too much, bring it to the boil and reduce. Soak the gelatine in a small bowl of cold water to soften, then remove and squeeze out the excess liquid. Add the gelatine to the hot stock and stir well to melt.

Cut the gammon into small bite-sized cubes and place them in a bowl. Leave some or all of the fat and skin, as it is delicious.

When the cooking liquid is semi-set and has the consistency of cream, add the chopped parsley, tarragon vinegar and nutmeg, season with black pepper and mix with the gammon. Pour all of this into a large glass bowl or terrine, cover and refrigerate overnight.

Turn the terrine out on to a plate to enjoy its full splendour or spoon out wedges to serve with plenty of toasted country style bread and mustard.

SERVES 12

900g good-quality green gammon leg meat, off the bone and preferably with some skin and fat
½ pig's trotter, split
325ml dry white wine
6 whole black peppercorns
3 juniper berries
1 bunch of flatleaf parsley
1 bunch of tarragon
1 sprig of thyme

JELLY

3 leaves of gelatine
1 bunch of flatleaf parsley, chopped
1 tbsp tarragon vinegar
grating of nutmeg
black pepper

Terrine de poireaux au fromage de chèvre

LEEK TERRINE WITH GOAT'S CHEESE

This is a very simple but effective vegetable terrine that makes a lovely light starter with some goat's cheese or the goat's cheese cream suggested here. If you can't find goat's curd, use a soft goat's cheese and mash it with the crème fraiche.

SERVES 12—14

salt

pinch of sugar

20 medium leeks, trimmed, washed and left whole

GOAT'S CHEESE CREAM

180g soft goat's curd

100g crème fraiche

1 tbsp chopped chives

olive oil

salt

black pepper

Bring a large pan of water to the boil and season with a generous amount of salt and a little sugar. Add the leeks and cook them for 10–12 minutes or until tender. Check with the point of a knife – it should pierce the leeks easily. When the leeks are ready, carefully remove them from the pan and drain them on a rack so they keep their shape.

Line a terrine dish measuring about 24 x 8cm with a double layer of cling film, leaving plenty of cling film overlapping the sides. Place the whole leeks in the terrine, arranging them head to tail so you get alternating strips of green and white in the terrine. Wrap the overlapping cling film tightly over the top and pierce it a few times with the point of a knife.

Now you need to weigh down the terrine to press out the excess water. The ideal way of doing this is to place another terrine of exactly the same size inside the first dish and weigh that down with heavy weights. Alternatively, place a small board inside the terrine, covering the leeks, and put a weight on top. It does need to be really heavy to press out the water. Place the whole thing on a tray to catch the water and leave in the fridge overnight.

The next day, carefully turn the terrine out on to a serving dish and cut it into slices with a sharp knife. Serve with the goat's cheese cream or simply with a beautiful goat's cheese.

To make the goat's cheese cream, mash the goat's curd with the crème fraiche until smooth and light, then season with salt, pepper, chopped chives and a drizzle of olive oil.

Petit pâté de Pézenas

SWEET MUTTON PIES

These little sweet, spicy mutton pies were first introduced to France by Clive of India, who ordered his servants to cook them when he stayed near the village of Pézenas in the Languedoc-Roussillon region. The pies caught on and have become a classic dish. It is essential to get the right balance of sweet, salty and spicy flavours so check the seasoning carefully. The size and shape of a cotton reel, the pies make a lovely starter for a special meal or could be served with salad as a light lunch.

Make the pastry first, as it needs to rest before use. Mix the flour and salt in a bowl, then work in the butter with your fingertips. Add the water and bring the pastry into a ball. Wrap it in cling film and leave it in the fridge to rest for 30 minutes.

Check that you've removed all the sinew and gristle from the lamb or mutton and chop the meat with the kidney fat to make a coarse mixture. Season with the spices, sugar and salt and pepper and add the lemon zest. Quickly fry a tiny piece of the mixture and taste it to make sure that you have the right balance of flavours.

Roll out the pastry until it is quite thin and cut out 5 strips measuring 20 x 6cm, then cut 10 discs of 6cm across for the tops and bases. Take a pastry disc, place it on a baking tray and arrange a strip on top, shaping it round like a cotton reel. Use a little beaten egg or water to seal the edge in place. Repeat to make 4 more little pastry cases.

Preheat the oven to 220°C/Fan 200°C/Gas 7. Carefully fill each pastry case with the meat mixture and top with a pastry disc. Use a little beaten egg or water to stick down the edges and then make a little incision on the top. Cook the pies in the preheated oven for about 20 minutes until golden and cooked through. Serve warm with a salad.

MAKES 5 PIES

PASTRY
250g flour
2 pinches of salt
100g cold unsalted butter, diced
125ml water
beaten egg or water

FILLING
250g lamb or mutton shoulder, trimmed
100g lamb kidney fat
pinch each of cumin and cinnamon
grating of nutmeg
½ tsp demerara sugar
grated zest of 1 lemon
salt
black pepper

Tête de porc et sa salade aux noisettes

PIG'S HEAD WITH HAZELNUT SALAD

This is a perfect example of something very delicious made with parts of an animal that some might think inedible. It's best served not too cold so remember to take the dish out of the fridge for a while before serving.

Place the cleaned pig's head and cheeks in a large pan with the onion, celery, carrot and herbs. Cover with cold water, add salt and bring to a very gentle simmer. Continue to simmer for 2 hours or until the meat is tender. Leave to cool in the liquid.

When the head is cool enough to handle, take it out of the pan, keeping the cooking liquid. Bring the cooking liquid to the boil again and cook until reduced. Carefully remove the bones from the head and lay one half, skin-side down, on a tray lined with cling film. Pick the meat off the skin from both halves of the head and shred, then shred the cheek and tongue meat. Add the sliced ears, then season well with salt and pepper and moisten with a little of the reduced cooking liquor.

Spread this mixture on top of the skin and place the other half, skin-side up, on top. Cover with cling film, place some weights on top and leave in the fridge to set.

To make the garnish, roast the shallots in their skins at 200°C/Fan 180°C/Gas 6 for 30 minutes. Remove the skins and blitz the flesh until smooth to make a purée.

Whisk the honey, vinegar and mustard with the oil to make the dressing, then season lightly with salt and pepper. Mix the leaves with the hazelnuts and apple sticks and drizzle with the dressing.

Cut the pig's head into slices and serve with the salad, shallot purée and some bread or toasted baguette rubbed with a cut clove of garlic.

SERVES 10—12

1 pig's head, including tongue, split in half
4 pig cheeks
1 onion, peeled and roughly chopped
1 celery stick, roughly chopped
1 carrot, peeled and roughly chopped
2 bay leaves
1 sprig of thyme
salt
black pepper

GARNISH

4 shallots
½ tbsp clear honey
1 tbsp sherry vinegar
½ tbsp grain mustard
4 tbsp hazelnut oil
mixed baby leaves
60g toasted hazelnuts, crushed
1 green apple, cut into matchsticks
salt
black pepper

Caillettes de porc aux herbes

PORK LIVER PARCELS WITH HERBS

Every butcher and charcutier makes their own version
of these delicious little meaty parcels and I can't think
of another dish that's found in so many parts of France.
When you've nothing in the fridge, you can pop round
the corner to buy some caillettes and serve them hot or
cold for an instant snack or meal – they are so versatile.
Some recipes include some chard, spinach or sorrel
leaves in the mixture. If you do this, you need to cook
the leaves gently in a little oil until tender, then drain
them and squeeze out any excess water before adding
them to the meat.

SERVES 4

200g pig's liver
250g pork fat
100g pork shoulder
2 garlic cloves, peeled and
    chopped
120g mixed herbs such as
    chives, sage and parsley,
    chopped
2 shallots, peeled and
    chopped
160g pork caul fat
salt
black pepper

Mince the liver, pork fat and shoulder, then mix in the garlic, herbs and
shallots. Season the mixture well. If using chard, spinach or sorrel, cook
them as above and add to the meat mixture at this stage. Preheat the oven
to 200°C/Fan 180°C/Gas 6.

Rinse the caul fat and lay it out on the work surface. Divide the meat into
4 or 5 balls and place them on the caul fat. Wrap the meatballs individually
in the fat, tearing it as you go, and place them in an ovenproof dish – they
should fit tightly. Bake in the preheated oven for 30 minutes.

You can serve these hot or cold, as a main dish or a snack. I like them cold
with some hot toasted or grilled bread, drizzled with olive oil.

Dans le cochon, tout est bon

Everything in a pig is good
GRIMOD DE LA REYNIÈRE

Foie gras rôti aux raisins

ROAST FOIE GRAS WITH RAISINS

A speciality of southwest France, foie gras is
particularly good served with a local sweet wine such
as Barsac or Sauternes. Be sure to keep the fat that is
rendered as the liver cooks and use it in another dish.

SERVES 4 AS A STARTER OR
2–3 AS A MAIN COURSE

30 seedless white grapes
60g golden raisins
60ml dry white wine
60ml marc de Bourgogne
    (or grappa)
1 whole duck foie gras (450g)
2 shallots, peeled and finely
    chopped
1 tbsp caster sugar
2 tbsp sherry vinegar
200ml duck stock
salt
black pepper

To peel the grapes, plunge them into a pan of boiling water for a few
seconds, then remove and refresh in iced water. Using a sharp knife, gently
remove the skins and put the grapes in a bowl. Blanch the raisins in boiling
water for 30 seconds, then drain and add them to the bowl with the grapes.
Pour in the white wine and marc or grappa and leave the grapes and raisins
to marinate for at least a couple of hours.

Preheat the oven to 220°C/Fan 200°C/Gas 7. Break the duck foie gras into
2 natural pieces and remove any obvious nerves, blemishes or green stains
from the gall bladder, which may be bitter. Season the liver well, place it in
a cold ovenproof pan and put it into the hot oven. Cook for 10 minutes, then
turn the liver over and baste it with the rendered fat. Continue to cook until
the smaller of the lobes of foie gras is firm to touch and cooked through; this
should be no more than 15 minutes in total. Remove and leave to rest in a
warm place while the larger lobe cooks for a further 10 minutes. Place it with
the smaller one, drain off the fat into a bowl and store in the fridge.

Using the same pan, sweat the shallots until translucent, then add the sugar
and vinegar. Cook for a couple of minutes, then add the marinade from
the grapes and raisins and boil until reduced to a glaze. Add the stock and
reduce again until it has the consistency of a sauce. Pour this over the grapes
and raisins and serve hot with the liver.

Rillettes de lapin

RABBIT RILLETTES

Rillettes can be made from many different meats but this recipe is one of my favourites. You can vary the seasoning if you like by adding ingredients such as green peppercorns or toasted pistachios. I like to serve these rillettes straight from a glass parfait jar, but if you are feeling in the mood for something fancy, shape them into neat quenelles with a tablespoon.

Cut the pork back fat into small cubes, put these in a large saucepan and cover with plenty of water – about 2 litres. Simmer for about an hour, until the fat has softened and become translucent, and the water has evaporated. Add the bouquet garni, onion, carrot, garlic, bacon and 375ml of the white wine. Season generously with salt, pepper and a grating of nutmeg – when cold, the rillettes will taste bland if not slightly over seasoned now.

Add the rabbit and diced pork to the pan and stir well. Cover with a piece of baking parchment paper and turn down the heat so the mixture is barely simmering. Cook for about 2 hours, stirring occasionally, until the meat is so soft that it crumbles.

Take the pan off the heat and pour the mixture into a clean bowl set over ice. Add 200ml more wine and stir vigorously with a spatula until cold. The rillette mixture will change colour and turn opaque-white from the emulsified fat. Put the rillettes into jars or a terrine dish and store in the fridge. It will keep for 2–3 weeks. Serve with hot toast and cornichons.

SERVES 15–20

1.2kg pork back fat

about 2 litres water

bouquet garni, made up of celery, leek, 2 bay leaves, parsley stalks and thyme (see page 342)

1 onion, peeled and studded with 2 cloves

1 carrot, peeled

3 garlic cloves, peeled

150g smoked bacon, diced

1 bottle of dry white wine

freshly grated nutmeg

1.2kg whole rabbit (not wild), boned and cut up

400g pork shoulder, cut into large dice

salt

black pepper

Terrine de poisson

FISH TERRINE

This recipe does make a large terrine but it keeps for
a week in the fridge and can be served hot or cold.
The beautiful green colour comes from the natural
chlorophyll in the green leaves – a trick I learned from
my father and not known to many chefs nowadays.

Blitz the 500 grams of white fish in a blender with the egg whites to make a
smooth purée. Pass this through a fine drum sieve into a bowl, making sure
you scrape all the mixture off the base of the sieve. Place the bowl over ice
and gently beat in enough cream to make it the consistency of mayonnaise.
You may not need all the cream so add it in stages. Season well, then test
the mousse for texture and taste. To do this, bring a small pan of seasoned
water to simmering point and drop in a teaspoon of mousse. Cook for 3–4
minutes, then taste and add more cream or seasoning if necessary.

Butter a terrine measuring about a 31 x 12 x 10.5cm. Bring a pan of water
to the boil and add enough large spinach leaves to line the terrine. Drain
immediately and plunge the leaves into cold water, then use them to line the
terrine, leaving no gaps and letting them hang over the edge of the dish.

Blitz the remaining spinach with the watercress and parsley and enough
water to make a wet mulch. Press this through a fine strainer to extract all
the liquid. Put this liquid in a pan on a medium heat, being careful not to let
it boil or the chlorophyll will loose its vibrant colour. Skim the solid matter
floating on the top and drain it on a muslin cloth – this is the chlorophyll.

Spoon half of the mousse into another bowl and add enough chlorophyll
to colour it green. Beat out the sole or plaice fillets to flatten them slightly
and lay them in a row on cling film. Season, then spread some of the white
mousse over them. Lay a thick strip (2–3cm) of salmon over the mousse
and roll it all up. Add a layer of white mousse to the terrine, then add the
white fish and salmon roll. Finish with alternating layers of green and white
mousse and fold the spinach over the top. Cover with buttered foil.

Preheat the oven to 160°C/Fan 140°C/Gas 3. Put the terrine in a roasting tin,
pour in enough boiling water to come halfway up the sides, then bake for 1½
hours. Remove and leave to cool completely before slicing. Serve cold with
herb mayonnaise (see page 333) or warm with beurre blanc (see page 332).
If serving warm, gently reheat the slices in a steamer.

SERVES 14–16

500g fillets of white fish,
  such as whiting, skinned
  and pin bones removed
3 free-range egg whites
up to 750g double cream
unsalted butter, for greasing
200g large leaf spinach,
  washed and stalks removed
1 bunch of watercress
1 bunch of curly parsley
6 large fillets of sole or plaice
300g fresh salmon
salt
black pepper

*La cuisine c'est beaucoup
plus que des recettes*

Cooking is much more than recipes

ALAIN CHAPEL

Mousse de jambon

HAM MOUSSE

This really is a step back in time, when grand
cuisine was all about mousses, jellies and elaborate
decorations. But with a light, delicate, modern touch
this classic recipe definitely deserves a comeback. The
truffle is an extravagance but really does finish the dish.

To make the béchamel, bring the milk to the boil with the clove-studded
onion, bay leaf and seasoning. Cover and set aside. Gently melt the butter
in a small pan and stir in the flour, then whisk and cook for 3–4 minutes
over a low heat. Strain the milk into the butter and flour, then whisk to get
rid of any lumps. Bring the sauce to the boil, then turn down the heat and
cook for 15 minutes. Dot with a little butter to avoid a skin foaming.

Trim any fat and sinew off the ham, then purée it in a food processor with
200g of the béchamel sauce until smooth. Melt 300ml of the jelly in a pan,
setting the rest aside for later. Add the melted jelly to the mixture in the
processor with the whipped cream, a grating of nutmeg and salt and pepper.
Process until smooth. For a super-fine mousse, press the mixture through
a fine sieve before adding the jelly, cream and seasoning.

Leave the mousse in the fridge overnight to set. When you're ready to serve,
dip 2 dessertspoons in hot water and shape the mousse into quenelles (neat
egg shapes). Decorate them with slices of hard-boiled egg white and truffle
and serve with the rest of the Madeira jelly and toasted brioche.

SERVES 8

350g best-quality cooked
  ham
400ml Madeira jelly
  (see page 336)
200ml double cream,
  whipped
freshly grated nutmeg
salt
black pepper

GARNISH

whites of 2 hard-boiled
  free-range eggs, sliced
1 truffle, sliced
toasted brioche

BÉCHAMEL SAUCE

500ml milk
1 white onion, peeled and
  studded with 2 cloves
1 bay leaf
50g unsalted butter, plus
  extra for dotting the
  surface
60g plain flour
salt
black pepper

Pâté de volaille et pistaches

CHICKEN AND PORK PÂTÉ WITH PISTACHIOS

This is what we call a *pâté grandmère*. It's a traditional country-style pâté and a great staple to have in the fridge for everyone to help themselves to whenever they want. In France there are 101 varieties of pâté and terrines, which can be made in anything from cake tins to parfait jars. I'm never without them. You can make this recipe with any poultry you like and use hazelnuts instead of pistachios if you prefer.

Cut each of the chicken supremes lengthways into 3 big slices and set them aside. Mix the chicken livers into the minced pork and season, then add the lemon zest, shallots, thyme and pistachios.

Line a mould, such as a 20cm cake tin or earthenware dish, with overlapping rashers of bacon, making sure it is completely covered and leaving some bacon hanging over the edges. Press in half the mince mixture, add the chicken pieces, then cover with the rest of the mince. Fold over the bacon rashers to encase the filling.

Preheat the oven to 200°C/Fan 180°C/Gas 6. Place the dish in a roasting tin and pour in enough boiling water to come about halfway up the sides. Bake for 45 minutes to 1 hour, depending on the size of the mould. Check that the pâté is done by piercing the centre with a needle. The juices should run clear and the needle should feel hot to the touch.

Allow to cool, then chill overnight in the fridge. Turn out and serve in slices with pickled onions or gherkins, toast and salad leaves.

SERVES 8

3 free-range chicken supremes, skinned
100g free-range chicken livers, trimmed
180g pork belly (fatty), minced
1½ tsp salt
2 tsp ground black pepper
grated zest of 1 unwaxed lemon
2 shallots, peeled and finely chopped
2 sprigs of lemon thyme, chopped
50g shelled pistachios (blanched)
20–25 thin rashers of streaky bacon, depending on the size of your mould

Cou de canard farci

STUFFED DUCK NECK

This is a traditional way of using duck necks in southwest France and is usually served cold with a little salad or some radishes. Alternatively, Cumberland sauce, that great British accompaniment for cold cuts, also goes well.

The duck necks should be as long as possible and have no holes. Remove the neck bones, sinew and excess fat. Using butcher's string, tie each neck at the thin end ready for stuffing.

Chop the meat, fat and foie gras into 1cm dice. Mince a third of this as finely as possible, then fold it into the rest of the meat. Add the thyme leaves, pistachios and truffle and season with the coriander, salt and pepper. Pour the duck stock into a small pan and reduce it to a sticky syrup, then fold it into the mixture.

Push the stuffing into the necks, making sure there are no air pockets, and tie the ends securely with butcher's string. Take a pan that's big enough for the duck necks to lie flat, add water and a pinch of salt. Heat the water to 70°C, then add the duck necks and poach them gently for 40 minutes.

Take the pan off the heat and leave the necks to cool a little, then remove them and refrigerate. They are best left to mature for 48 hours before slicing and serving, and they keep well for a couple of weeks in the fridge.

SERVES 10 AS A STARTER

2 duck necks
500g duck meat, cleaned
    of fat and sinew
120g pork back fat
350g cooked foie gras
2 tsp chopped thyme leaves
60g pistachios (shelled
    weight), chopped
60g cooked truffle, chopped
pinch of ground coriander
250ml duck stock
    (see page 322)
salt
black pepper

Cheese and eggs make a wonderful marriage, but cheese on its own is truly delicious. No meal in France, however casual, is complete without a little cheese. For me, eggs are the simplest and most satisfying of fast food. They are so versatile, used in everything from the quickest snack to the most elaborate recipes. And eggs are not just an ingredient in French cooking – they can be the focal point of many recipes and have inspired some great classics. There's nothing as French as a perfect omelette.

Oeufs et fromage

Croque monsieur

TOASTED HAM AND CHEESE SANDWICH

Properly made with béchamel sauce, this classic French hot sandwich is a delight but it is all too easy to find disappointing versions. Try preparing your own to enjoy the croque in its full glory.

Lightly toast the bread on both sides, then butter one side of each slice.

To make the béchamel sauce, melt the remaining butter in a small pan, stir in the flour to make a roux, then whisk in the milk. Keep whisking it well to avoid lumps and bring the sauce to the boil. Season with salt, pepper and nutmeg and cook for 3–4 minutes, then remove from the heat.

Preheat the oven to 200°C/Fan 180°C/Gas 6. Spread a little mustard on the buttered side of a piece of toast. Add a generous amount of béchamel, followed by grated cheese and a slice of ham. Spread some more béchamel on the dry side of another piece of toast and place on top of the ham, pressing a little to stick it down. Spread a little more béchamel on top of the sandwich and sprinkle with grated cheese. Make all the sandwiches in the same way.

Put the sandwiches on a baking tray and bake them in the preheated oven for 6–8 minutes until crisp and golden. Serve at once.

SERVES 4

8 slices of good sourdough bread
2 tbsp unsalted butter
1 tbsp plain flour
400ml milk
freshly grated nutmeg
Dijon mustard
280g grated cheese (a mixture of Emmental, Gruyère and Cheddar is good)
160g good-quality, sliced ham
salt
black pepper

Tartiflette

CHEESE AND POTATO BAKE

A classic from the Haute-Savoie region in the French Alps, tartiflette is a hearty dish that has become a favourite on bistro menus. It's simple to prepare and makes a good lunch on a cold winter's day.

Peel the potatoes and cut them into large dice. Wash in cold water, then put them in a pan of salted water and bring to the boil. Cook for 3 minutes, then drain well.

Cut the ventrèche into lardons and put them in a large frying pan with a dash of vegetable oil. Gently fry the lardons until the fat starts running, then add the potatoes. Continue to cook for 5–6 minutes, stirring occasionally and scraping the pan if necessary, until the potatoes have taken on a little colour. Preheat the oven to 220°C/Fan 200°C/Gas 7.

Season the potatoes and tip everything into an ovenproof dish. Scatter the chopped cheese on top and bake in the hot oven for 15 minutes. Finish under a preheated grill to brown the top.

SERVES 6

1kg potatoes (Roosters or Desiree)
260g ventrèche or dry-cured bacon
vegetable oil
500g Reblochon cheese, chopped
salt
black pepper

Oeufs brouillés Alexandra

SCRAMBLED EGGS WITH CHOUX BUNS AND CHICKEN

I love scrambled eggs, the creamier the better, and I'll
eat them at any time of day as a starter or a main meal.
I first came across this rather special version when
working at the Élysée Palace for President Mitterrand.

First make the choux buns. Preheat the oven to 240°C/Fan 220°C/Gas 9.
Pour the water and milk into a pan, add the butter, salt and sugar and bring
to the boil. Take the pan off the heat and beat in the flour. Once all the
flour has been incorporated put the pan back on the heat and cook for 6–7
minutes, stirring continuously. Take the pan off the heat again and beat in
4 of the eggs, one at a time, and mix until smooth. The mixture might look
as though it is splitting but keep beating and it will all come together.

Put the mixture into a piping bag and pipe 24 little rounds on to a non-stick
baking sheet, taking care to keep them all about the same size and shape so
they cook evenly. Beat the remaining egg and use it to brush the buns, then
bake them for 5 minutes. Open the oven door to release the steam, turn the
temperature down to 200°C/Fan 180°C/Gas 6 and cook for another 12–15
minutes or until crisp and cooked. Remove and place on a rack to cool.

Season the chicken supremes with salt and pepper. Heat the butter in a
frying pan until foaming and fry the chicken until golden on both sides and
very pink inside. Take the chicken out of the pan and discard the butter.
Deglaze the pan with the port, then cook to reduce by half. Add the chicken
jus and reduce to a sauce consistency. Cut the chicken into small dice, put it
back in the sauce and continue to cook until done.

Now for the eggs. Use all the butter to grease a thick-based saucepan, then
add the beaten eggs and cook over a medium heat while stirring with a
spatula. When the eggs are almost completely cooked, season and pour in
the double cream.

To serve, cut the tops off the choux buns and fill them three-quarters full
with scrambled eggs, followed by the chicken mixture. Place the lids back
on top and serve immediately.

SERVES 8 AS A STARTER

CHOUX BUNS (MAKES 24)

125ml water

125ml milk

100g unsalted butter

1 pinch of salt

2 pinches of sugar

150g flour

5 free-range eggs

CHICKEN

2 free-range chicken
    supremes, skinned

1 tbsp unsalted butter

30ml port

200ml chicken jus

salt

black pepper

EGGS

2 tbsp unsalted butter

16 free-range eggs, beaten

100ml double cream

salt

black pepper

Oeufs friands

SCRAMBLED EGGS WITH WOODCOCK

This was originally eaten as a savoury at the end of a
meal, but I like to serve it as a starter or lunch dish or
even as a light main course. Traditionally this recipe
was served in puff pastry vol-au-vents, but I prefer the
toasted brioche, which adds a little richness and texture
to this extravagant, luxurious delight.

Prepare the woodcock for roasting and remove the guts – or ask your butcher
to do this for you. Set the upper intestines, heart and liver aside for later,
but discard the gizzard which will be full of gravel. Season the woodcock and
push the beak through the legs to hold it in place.

Preheat the oven to 220°C/Fan 200°C/Gas 7. Heat the oil in a roasting
pan on top of the stove, add the woodcock and brown them briefly. Add a
tablespoon of the butter and heat until it is foaming but not burnt, then put
the pan of woodcock in the hot oven for no more than 8 minutes – the meat
should still be very pink. Leave to rest in a warm place.

Drain the fat from the roasting pan and discard, then add another
tablespoon of butter to the pan and heat it on the hob. When the butter is
hot, add the chopped shallot and garlic, cook for 30 seconds, then add the
woodcock entrails and chicken livers. Season well and cook over a high heat
for 2 minutes until cooked pink, then add the brandy and flambé. Press the
mixture through a fine sieve, then spread it over the toasted brioche and
keep warm. Remove the breasts from the woodcock and split each head in
half along the beak.

Grease a heavy-based pan with the remaining butter, then add the eggs and
cook over a medium heat while stirring with a spatula. When the eggs are
almost completely cooked, season and add the double cream. Keep them
nice and creamy – don't overcook them. Serve the eggs with the brioche,
a woodcock breast and half a head. Add a little game jus, if you like.

SERVES 4

2 woodcock
1 tbsp vegetable oil
3 tbsp unsalted butter
1 shallot, peeled and finely
    chopped
½ garlic clove, peeled and
    finely chopped
2 free-range chicken livers
1 tbsp brandy
4 thick slices of brioche
    lightly toasted and
    crusts removed
8 free-range eggs, beaten
2 tbsp double cream
game jus (optional – see
    page 329)
salt
black pepper

Omelette aux girolles

OMELETTE WITH GIROLLE MUSHROOMS

Omelettes are an essential in the French kitchen and everyone has a favourite version. During the wild mushroom season a *poelé* of girolles with just a hint of new season garlic and parsley makes the humble omelette into a feast fit for a prince. Then comes the truffle season and a truffle omelette is food for a king. Another of my favourites is with grated goat's cheese, especially the Pélardon cheese from the Cévennes. It's so dry that it is impossible to bite into, but when grated into a perfectly *baveuse* omelette it's heavenly.

SERVES 2

4 free-range eggs (or 6 if greedy)
100g girolle mushrooms or any wild mushrooms, such as morels or ceps
vegetable oil
½ garlic clove, peeled and finely chopped
1 tbsp finely chopped parsley
2 tbsp unsalted butter
salt
black pepper

Crack the eggs into a bowl, beat them with a fork and season with salt and pepper. Trim and wipe the mushrooms, then fry them in a little oil and add the finely chopped garlic and parsley. Season and set aside.

Heat a 20cm omelette pan until it's very hot, then add a drop of oil and the butter. The butter should be golden but don't let it burn. Pour in the eggs and leave the pan for 20 seconds or so before starting to mix them with a fork or spatula. Once the omelette has formed and is holding but still a little underdone, add the mushrooms in the centre and carefully roll the omelette over them to the edge of the pan.

Flip the omelette on to a warm plate and cut it in half to serve. It should have a little colour but be light and fluffy – brush with a little butter to give it a lovely shine and gloss.

Soufflé aux épinards

SPINACH SOUFFLÉ

This is not hard to do and once you've mastered the technique, a soufflé is an impressive dish. You'll need four ramekins measuring 8 x 6cm if making individual soufflés or one 20cm dish. The béchamel sauce recipe makes more than you need for the soufflé but it keeps in the fridge for a week. Cover it well, though.

Bring a pan of salted water to the boil and blanch the spinach for 30 seconds. Plunge it into iced water to refresh, then drain and press out some of the water with your hands. Blitz the spinach in a food processor until smooth, then place it in a clean cloth and press and squeeze out as much water as you can until the spinach purée is as dry as possible.

To make the béchamel, melt the butter in a small pan. Stir in the flour and cook for 3–4 minutes without letting it colour, then whisk in the milk. Bring to the boil and whisk until the sauce is smooth. Season with a grating of nutmeg and some salt and pepper, then cover to avoid a skin forming.

Preheat the oven to 200°C/Fan 180°C/Gas 6. Butter your ramekins or mould and coat the insides with grated Parmesan. Put 4 tablespoons of béchamel in a bowl, add 4 tablespoons of the spinach and mix well with the 2 egg yolks. Whisk the egg whites in a separate bowl with a pinch of salt until stiff, then fold into the béchamel and spinach mixture until smooth. Do not over mix.

Pour the mixture into the ramekins or mould and level off the top with a spatula. Run a knife or your thumb around the inside rim to ensure a straight rise. Place in the preheated oven and cook for 8–10 minutes for individual souffles or 16–18 minutes for the bigger one. Serve immediately on its own or with a sauce such as tomato coulis (see page 336).

SERVES 4

400g leaf spinach
unsalted butter, for greasing
60g Parmesan cheese, grated
2 medium free-range egg
    yolks
8 medium free-range egg
    whites
pinch of salt

BÉCHAMEL SAUCE

40g unsalted butter
40g flour
200ml milk
freshly grated nutmeg
salt
black pepper

Surtout, faites simple

Above all, keep it simple

AUGUSTE ESCOFFIER

Poireaux vinaigrette aux oeufs

LEEK SALAD EGG VINAIGRETTE

Make this simple French classic with young tender leeks for a perfect lunch or starter.

Trim off the dark green tops of the leeks, leaving about 3cm of the light green. Bring a large pan of salted water to the boil, add the leeks and cook them until tender – this should take about 6 minutes. Drain the leeks and lay them flat on a rack to cool slightly while you make the vinaigrette.

Put the mustard, vinegar and seasoning in a bowl with a little of the water. Whisk as if making a mayonnaise, slowly adding the oil to emulsify the vinaigrette. Add a little more water if the mixture becomes too thick.

Cut the leeks in half lengthways and arrange them on a dish or plate. Scatter over the chopped egg and snipped chives. Drizzle with the vinaigrette and eat while the leeks are still warm.

SERVES 4

16 young leeks, washed
2 free-range eggs, hard-
    boiled and chopped
1 bunch of chives, snipped
salt
black pepper

VINAIGRETTE

2 tbsp Dijon mustard
2 tbsp red wine vinegar
4–6 tbsp water
300ml vegetable or
    peanut oil

Oeufs pochés à la Rossini

POACHED EGGS WITH TRUFFLE AND MADEIRA SAUCE

Sheer extravagance, this recipe is as old as the more well known tournedos Rossini. Both were created by Antonin Carême, one of the most famous 19th century French chefs, in honour of the Italian composer Rossini, who famously loved his food. Both are rich, luxurious dishes fit for a special occasion.

First make the sauce. Put the shallots in a saucepan with the sliced mushrooms and a little of the butter and cook over a medium heat until the shallots are caramelised. Then add the port and Madeira, bring to the boil and cook until reduced by half. Add the stock and truffle juice and simmer for 20 minutes until syrupy, skimming regularly.

Remove the pan from the heat and pass the sauce through a fine sieve, pressing well to extract as much flavour as possible. Cut the remaining butter into cubes. Pour the sauce back into the pan, bring it to the boil and add the cubes of cold butter to thicken the sauce and give it a lustre. Season with salt and pepper and a few drops of vinegar to balance the sweetness, then set aside and keep warm.

Cut the brioche into rounds of about 8cm and trim the slices of foie gras terrine to fit – devour the trimmings as you do this. Warm the clarified butter in a pan and lightly fry the brioche slices. Drain and set aside.

Bring a pan of water to the boil and add the vinegar. This helps to set the white part of the egg so that it has an elegant shape – salting the water has the opposite effect. Crack the eggs into separate bowls. Swirl the water with a spoon, gently add the eggs and poach for 5 minutes or until cooked but with soft yolks. Carefully remove the eggs with a slotted spoon.

While the eggs are cooking, place a slice of foie gras on each piece of brioche. If necessary, you could warm these briefly in the oven at 180°C/Fan 160°C/Gas 4. Trim the eggs neatly and place them on top of the foie gras. Decorate with thin slices of truffle and serve with the sauce.

If you'd like to get everything ready in advance to put together at the last minute, poach the eggs, then refresh them in iced water and set aside. When you're ready to serve, reheat the eggs for 30 seconds in a steamer over a pan of simmering water.

SERVES 4

4 thin slices of brioche
4 slices of cooked foie gras
2 tbsp clarified butter
    (see page 330)
1 tbsp white wine vinegar
4 duck eggs
1 x 50g black truffle

SAUCE

2 shallots, peeled and sliced
6 button mushrooms, wiped
    and sliced
2 tbsp cold unsalted butter
125ml port
125ml Madeira wine
500ml veal stock
    (see page 322)
2 tbsp truffle juice (available
    in cans)
sherry vinegar
salt
black pepper

Oeufs cocotte au maïs et chorizo

BAKED EGGS WITH CORN AND CHORIZO

Eggs cooked in little pots – en cocotte – like this are
a popular classic in France and simple and quick to
prepare. This version makes a lovely starter or light
meal at any time.

Preheat the oven to 200°C/Fan 180°C/Gas 6. Take 4 small ovenproof dishes,
such as ramekins, and lightly butter the insides.

Pour a tablespoon of cream into each dish, followed by some drained
sweetcorn and a few slices of chorizo. Then carefully crack an egg into each
dish, lightly season with salt and pepper and then cover with more cream
so the yolk can only just be seen. Season again, then place the dishes in a
roasting tin and pour in enough boiling water to come halfway up the sides.
Bake in the preheated oven for 6 minutes or until the egg whites have set but
the yolks are still runny.

Sprinkle the eggs with a little paprika and serve immediately with some
toast soldiers.

SERVES 4

unsalted butter, for greasing
360ml double cream
125g can of sweetcorn
60g chorizo, sliced
4 free-range eggs
paprika
toast soldiers, for serving
salt
black pepper

Oeufs pochés meurette

POACHED EGGS IN A RED WINE SAUCE

This Burgundian dish was another recipe I first
encountered when I was working at the Élysée Palace
in Paris during my military service. It was President
Mitterrand's favourite – he liked it for breakfast.
You need a good strong red wine – preferably from
Burgundy of course.

SERVES 4

4 free-range eggs
1 bottle of strong red wine
200g smoked bacon (in one
    piece)
300ml veal stock
    (see page 322)
pinch of sugar
125g unsalted butter
12 cocktail onions, peeled
2 shallots, peeled and finely
    chopped
250g button mushrooms,
    wiped and finely chopped
50ml double cream
2 tbsp clarified butter
    (see page 330)
4 thick slices of brioche
salt
black pepper

Crack the eggs into separate cups. Bring the red wine to the boil in a large
pan. Stir to get the wine swirling, then carefully slip in the eggs and poach
them for 4 minutes or until cooked but with soft yolks. Remove the eggs with
a slotted spoon and place them in iced water to refresh, then set aside until
later. Keep the wine for the sauce.

Preheat the oven to 200°C/Fan 180°/Gas 6. Cut 4 thin slices from the bacon,
place them on a baking tray and cover with another baking tray. Cook in the
preheated oven until crisp. Put the rest of the bacon in a pan of cold water,
bring to the boil and simmer for 10 minutes, then cut into small lardons and
set aside.

Pour 250ml of the red wine into a pan and boil to reduce to a sticky glaze.
Then add the stock and reduce again until it has the consistency of a sauce.
Season with salt, pepper and a pinch of sugar if necessary, then add a little
of the butter to shine the sauce.

Melt a knob of butter in a frying pan, add the onions and cook them until
tender. Add a little of the sauce to glaze.

Sweat the chopped shallots and mushrooms in butter until cooked, then
season with salt and pepper. Add the cream and continue to cook until the
mixture is thick. Pan-fry the bacon lardons until golden.

Cut the brioche into 5cm circles and fry in the clarified butter until golden
but not dry. Drain and set aside.

Now, put everything together. Gently reheat the eggs in a steamer over
simmering water for about 3 minutes until warm but not overcooked. Place
each egg on a slice of brioche on warm plates. Add neat spoonfuls of the
mushroom mixture, lardons, onions and crispy bacon, then spoon on some
sauce. Serve immediately.

Oeufs pochés Carême

POACHED EGGS WITH SALMON AND ARTICHOKE HEARTS

Another classic created by Carême, this time for the
French royal family. For an even more luxurious dish,
top each one with a slice or two of truffle.

Peel off the leaves from each artichoke to reveal the heart. Trim to make the
hearts a perfect round shape and remove the chokes with a teaspoon (see
page 342). Bring a pan of salted water to the boil, add the artichoke hearts
with a little vinegar to keep them white and cook for about 15 minutes until
they are tender. Remove and set aside.

Crack the eggs into separate bowls. Bring a pan of water with a dash of
vinegar to a rolling boil, then swirl the water with a spoon, gently add the
eggs and poach them 3–4 minutes. Refresh the eggs in iced water, then
drain and trim.

For the mayonnaise, beat the egg in a bowl with the lemon juice and mustard
until smooth. Slowly add the vegetable oil in a thin steady stream, whisking
continuously. Stir in the cream, Tabasco and brandy.

Cut 2 circles of smoked salmon about the same size as the poached eggs.
Chop the rest and add it to the mayonnaise with the chopped chives. Season
with salt and pepper.

Fill the artichoke hearts with the salmon and mayonnaise mix. Top each with
the poached egg and a circle of smoked salmon, then serve at once.

SERVES 2

2 globe artichokes
white wine vinegar
2 free-range eggs
8 slices of smoked salmon
1 bunch of chives, chopped
salt
black pepper

MAYONNAISE

1 free-range egg
juice of ½ lemon
2 tsp Dijon mustard
100ml vegetable oil
1 tbsp cream
1 tsp Tabasco sauce
1 tsp brandy

I love to cook and eat fish and enjoy everything from the very simplest dishes to more elaborate recipes. I grew up eating fish on Fridays, and this Catholic tradition still prevails in much of rural France. Even if you're not religious, this is an excellent custom to keep up – and healthy too. Good-quality fish is available all over France, often in local markets. In central France they probably eat more freshwater species, while in Brittany and Normandy shellfish are the stars of many recipes. Salt cod is particularly popular in southern France. Good farmed fish, such as salmon, bream, bass, turbot and trout, is also available now at reasonable prices.

Poissons et fruits de mer

Huîtres Kilpatrick et huîtres Rockefeller

OYSTERS KILPATRICK AND OYSTERS ROCKEFELLER

Oysters are usually served raw in France, but sometimes
I like to make these two wonderful recipes for cooked
oysters. Kilpatrick is actually an Australian favourite,
and the shellfish are partnered with bacon and
breadcrumbs. Oysters Rockefeller are named after the
American billionaire, John D. Rockefeller, because the
creamy sauce is so rich!

Shuck all the oysters, collecting all the juice, and clean the bottom shells.

For oysters Kilpatrick, pour the oyster juice into a wide pan. Add the oysters,
bring to a simmer and cook for just a moment or two. Remove them and
set aside, keeping the poaching liquor. Fry the bacon, then stir it into the
breadcrumbs and set aside a quarter of the mixture for sprinkling on top of
the oysters. Mix the rest of the bacon and crumbs with the Worcestershire
and Tabasco sauces to taste, the lemon juice and enough of the poaching
liquor to make a thick sauce.

Divide this between the bottom shells and place the oysters on top. Sprinkle
with the reserved bacon and breadcrumb mixture and finish cooking under
a hot grill to brown and crisp the tops. Serve at once.

For oysters Rockefeller, blanch the spinach briefly in boiling water, then
refresh in cold water. Drain the spinach well, then squeeze out as much
water as possible and chop. Sweat the shallot in the butter, add the spinach,
chopped parsley and a dash of cream to moisten, then season with grated
nutmeg and pepper. Pour the oyster juice into a wide pan. Add the oysters,
bring to a simmer and cook for a moment or two, then remove them and set
aside, leaving the juices in the pan. Add a little pastis to the pan and reduce,
then add the rest of cream and reduce again until the mixture is thick and
creamy with the consistency of a sauce. Whisk in the egg yolk.

Place a little of the spinach mix into each bottom shell and top with an
oyster, then some sauce. Put the oysters under a preheated grill to bake and
glaze or into a preheated oven at 220°C/Fan 200°C/Gas 7 for a few minutes.
Serve the oysters hot on a bed of rock salt and seaweed.

SERVES 2

KILPATRICK
6 medium rock oysters
60g smoked bacon, finely
  diced
60g breadcrumbs
Worcestershire sauce
Tabasco sauce
juice of ½ lemon

ROCKEFELLER
6 medium rock oysters
100g spinach
1 shallot, peeled and chopped
½ tbsp unsalted butter
1 tbsp chopped flatleaf
  parsley
100ml double cream
freshly grated nutmeg
2 tsp pastis
1 free-range egg yolk
rock salt and seaweed, for
  serving
black pepper

Salade chaude de coques, palourdes et pommes de terre

WARM COCKLE, CLAM AND POTATO SALAD

In France we use a good red wine vinegar for this salad but malt vinegar, British seaside style, can also work well – in fact, I love it. The salad is a traditional dish from the tiny island of Noirmoutier, off the coast of the Vendée, where they grow a superb range of early potatoes. The crops are fertilised with seaweed, giving them a beautifully salty flavour.

Wash the cockles and clams well in cold water. Tip them into a very hot saucepan with a sliced shallot and the white wine. Cover and steam for 6–7 minutes until the shellfish have opened and are cooked. Drain and collect the cooking liquor.

Pour the liquor into a small pan, bring it to the boil and reduce by half. Strain the reduced liquid through a fine sieve and keep it warm.

Pick the meat from the cockles and clams, saving a few clam shells for decoration. Wash the potatoes and cook them in salted water. Peel them or not, as you prefer, and toss them while still warm with the cockles, clams, vinegar, oil and cooking liquor. Add the parsley and the remaining shallot, finely chopped, and sprinkle with a little piment d'Espelette before serving.

SERVES 4

1kg cockles
1kg Venus clams
2 shallots, peeled
250ml dry white wine
250g marble-sized potatoes, a mix of colours if you can find them
1 tbsp good red wine vinegar
4 tbsp olive oil
1 bunch of flatleaf parsley, finely chopped
ground piment d'Espelette (chilli powder)
salt

Dis-moi ce que tu manges, je te dirai qui tu es

Tell me what you eat, and I will tell you who you are

JEAN ANTHELME BRILLAT-SAVARIN

Ravioles de homard et St Jacques

PAN-FRIED LOBSTER AND SCALLOP RAVIOLI

This is my take on dim sum and uses a different sort of pasta dough to the normal kind. You can make the ravioli any shape you like, but they must contain the filling effectively and be well sealed, as they are fried briefly before serving.

First make the pasta dough. Put the flour in a bowl, add the remaining ingredients and knead to make an elastic, but not sticky, dough. Leave the dough to rest in the fridge for at least 20 minutes, then roll it out on the 'o' setting on a pasta machine.

Chop the scallops into 3mm dice. Break up the lobster, cutting the tail into quarters for the garnish. Extract all the rest of the lobster meat and cut into 5mm dice, then mix with the diced scallops and season with salt and a generous amount of pepper.

The shape of the ravioli is up to you, but the simplest method is to cut the pasta dough into 24 circles of about 6cm in diameter. Divide the scallop and lobster filling between 12 of the circles. Brush the borders with water to moisten, then top with the remaining circles and press down well around the edges to seal.

Bring a pan of salted water to the boil, add the ravioli and cook for 4 minutes. Remove the ravioli and plunge them into iced water to stop them cooking, then carefully drain and dry on a cloth and lightly drizzle them with olive oil. Keep the ravioli refrigerated until needed.

For the sauce, put the shallots, garlic and marjoram in a pan with the white wine and boil until the liquid has almost completely evaporated. Add the sundried tomatoes and lobster stock, then bring to the boil and simmer for 20 minutes. Pass the sauce through a fine sieve, then pour it back into the pan, season and finish with the cold butter to thicken and shine. Keep the sauce warm while you finish the ravioli.

Pan-fry the ravioli in a hot non-stick pan until golden on both sides and hot inside. Serve in warm bowls with the piping hot sauce and garnish with diced tomatoes and lobster claws and a few marjoram leaves.

SERVES 4

PASTA DOUGH
250g plain white flour
75g free-range egg whites
50g warm water
1 tbsp olive oil
pinch of salt

FILLING
8 large scallops (white meat only)
1 x 500g cooked lobster
olive oil
salt
black pepper

SAUCE
2 shallots, peeled and sliced
1 garlic clove, peeled and chopped
2 sprigs of marjoram
120ml dry white wine
6 sundried tomatoes (not in oil), chopped
500ml lobster stock (see page 325)
2 tbsp cold unsalted butter, cubed
salt
black pepper

GARNISH
4 tomatoes, peeled, deseeded and diced
marjoram leaves

Gratin de langoustines et escargots au piment d'Espelette

GRATIN OF LANGOUSTINES AND SNAILS WITH ESPELETTE PEPPER

This has long been a favourite on the menu at Le Gavroche and it's a French classic that we now make with British snails. There's quite a bit of work involved, as you need to make a hollandaise to enrich the creamy sauce, but it's well worth the effort.

First make the hollandaise. Put the vinegar, wine and water into a heavy-based pan and bring to the boil. Add a pinch of salt, remove the pan from the heat and leave to cool. Whisk in the egg yolks, then place the pan over a very gentle heat and keep whisking, making sure the whisk comes into contact with the whole base of the pan. After 8–10 minutes the yolks will have emulsified and you can increase the heat a little. The mixture should not exceed 68°C – if too hot the yolks will scramble – and should become smooth and thick enough to form peaks. Take the pan off the heat and whisk in the clarified butter, then cover and keep the sauce in a warm place for later.

Bring a pan of salted water to the boil, add the parsley and blanch for 4–5 minutes. Drain, keeping the water, then refresh the parsley in iced water. Drain it again well, pressing to extract excess water. Heat 100ml of the cream to boiling point. Put the parsley in a blender with a pinch of salt and the hot cream, then blitz until smooth, adding a little cooking water if needed.

Shell the langoustines and slice 2 of the shallots. Put the shallots in a pan with the wine and 6 of the langoustine heads, breaking them up with a spatula, then add a little salt and boil until the pan is almost dry. Add the stock and boil again until reduced by half, then add the rest of cream. Once the mixture has the consistency of a sauce, pass it through a fine sieve, then stir in the hollandaise and season with a little of the Espelette pepper. Set aside.

Chop the remaining shallot. Warm a teaspoon of the butter in a pan and add the snails with the shallot and garlic. Warm through, making sure you don't burn the garlic, then remove the snails and set them aside. Add the rest of the butter to the pan and heat until foaming. Toss the langoustines in the Espelette pepper, then add them to the pan to warm through. Preheat the grill. Take 8 heatproof bowls and add 3 snails, 3 langoustines and a little parsley purée to each one. Cover with the sauce, then place the bowls under the hot grill to glaze. Serve immediately.

SERVES 8

500g curly parsley, picked
    and washed
400ml double cream
24 cooked langoustines
3 large shallots, peeled
250ml dry white wine
300ml fish stock
    (see page 324)
½ tbsp ground piment
    d'Espelette (chilli powder)
2 tsp unsalted butter
24 cooked snails (canned or
    vacuum packed are fine)
2 garlic cloves, peeled and
    chopped
salt
black pepper

HOLLANDAISE SAUCE

1 tbsp white wine vinegar
3 tbsp white wine
2 tbsp water
4 free-range egg yolks
250g clarified butter
    (see page 330)
salt

Fricassée de homard au citron et noix de coco

LOBSTER WITH LEMON GRASS AND COCONUT BISQUE

Although this might not sound like a French dish,
it employs French classic techniques and has become
an indulgent favourite at Le Gavroche over the years.
We like to present it in the rather spectacular fashion
shown in the photograph opposite but if you prefer,
simply serve the pieces of lobster on the lemon purée
and pour in the warm bisque.

First make the lemon purée. Bring the sugar and water to the boil to make
the stock syrup and set it aside. Put the lemons in a pan of cold water, bring
to the boil, then drain. Repeat 10 times, adding fresh water each time, then
set them aside until cool enough to handle. Cut the lemons open and remove
any pips, then place them in a blender – skin and all –and purée until
smooth, adding some of the stock syrup to taste and a little salt. The purée
should be sharp so be careful not to add too much syrup. The purée sets
when it is cool and keeps well for several weeks.

Bring a huge pan of salted water to the boil, add the lobsters and cook them
for 4 minutes. Remove them from the pan and leave to cool. Once the
lobsters are cool enough to handle, take off their heads and set them aside.
Crack the bodies and claws, remove the flesh and cut it into into bite-sized
pieces. Keep the tails and tips of heads for garnishing the dish.

To make the bisque, put the remains of the lobsters (not the heads) in a pan
with any juices and a little olive oil. Add the chopped shallots, carrot, celery,
garlic, piment d'Espelette and lemon grass. Cook gently for 6–7 minutes,
then add the brandy and stir to deglaze the pan, followed by the white wine
and the mirin. Continue to cook until the liquid has almost evaporated,
then add the fish stock and tomato paste. Simmer for 20 minutes, then pass
through a fine sieve. Tip the soup back into the pan and boil to reduce the
liquid by half, then stir in the coconut cream and double cream.

Gently reheat the lobster meat in the melted butter and check the seasoning.
Serve the lobster on a bed of lemon purée with white asparagus or salsify
and slithers of fresh coconut, then pour in the warm bisque. I sometimes
like to serve this with some seaweed pasta as well (see page 339).

SERVES 4

4 x 500g uncooked lobsters
2 tbsp olive oil
2 shallots, peeled and
   chopped
1 carrot, peeled and chopped
1 celery stick, chopped
1 garlic clove, peeled and
   chopped
1 tsp flaked piment
   d'Espelette (dried chilli)
4 lemon grass sticks, crushed
2 tbsp brandy
250ml dry white wine
4 tbsp mirin paste
750ml fish stock
   (see page 324)
½ tbsp tomato paste
100ml coconut cream
60ml double cream
2 tbsp unsalted butter,
   melted
salt
black pepper

LEMON PURÉE

75g sugar
75ml water
5 unwaxed lemons (as fresh
   as possible)
salt

GARNISH

slivers of fresh coconut
cooked white asparagus or
   salsify

Flan aux moules et jus de homard

MUSSEL FLAN WITH LOBSTER JUS

These delightful little flans can be prepared a couple of hours ahead, then set aside in the fridge until you are nearly ready to eat. While you steam the flans you can reheat the lobster jus and warm the mussels through for a few seconds just before serving.

Wash the mussels and scrub them well. Warm a little oil in a large pan, add the shallots and cook them gently for a few moments. Add the thyme and crushed garlic, then the mussels and pour in the wine. Cover the pan with a lid and cook until all the mussels have opened, shaking the pan once or twice to toss them around.

Drain the mussels and set them aside, making sure you collect all the cooking juices – you should have about 300ml. Heat the cream and add the mussel cooking liquor, then take the pan off the heat and whisk in the whole eggs and the egg yolks. Pass this mixture through a fine sieve, check the seasoning, then pour it into 4 ramekins or similar heatproof dishes. Put these in a steamer over boiling water to cook for 10–15 minutes or until just set – they should be firm, like a crème brûlée. Alternatively, place the dishes in a roasting tin, pour in enough boiling water to come halfway up their sides and bake in a preheated oven, at 160°C/Fan 140°C/Gas 3, for about 20 minutes or until set.

Meanwhile, heat the lobster stock in a pan until reduced by half. Pick the mussels from the shells and cut the tomatoes into neat strips or petals. When the flans are cooked, arrange some mussels and pieces of tomato on the top of each dish and pour on the warm lobster stock.

SERVES 4 AS A STARTER

2kg mussels
olive oil
2 shallots, peeled and chopped
1 sprig of thyme
1 garlic clove, crushed
250ml dry white wine
200ml double cream
3 free-range eggs
3 free-range egg yolks
100ml lobster stock (see page 325)
2 ripe plum tomatoes, peeled and deseeded
salt
black pepper

Quiche au crabe

CRAB QUICHE

One of my favourite quiches, this is rich and full-flavoured with a touch of curry heat. I like to serve it with a little grilled endive – the slightly bitter smokiness sets off the sweetness of the crab perfectly. Use any kind of endive, such as Belgian or radicchio.

Start by making the pastry. Put the sifted flour on a clean, cold surface and make a well in the centre, then add the diced butter, egg and salt. Using your fingertips, work all the ingredients together, gradually drawing in the flour. Once the mixture has a sandy consistency, add the cold water and gently knead the pastry until smooth – but take care not to overwork it. Shape it into a ball, wrap in cling film and leave it to rest in the fridge for 2 hours.

Roll out the pastry on a floured surface to a circle about 3mm thick and use this to line a buttered 24cm flan ring. Leave the pastry to rest in the fridge again for at least 20 minutes. Preheat the oven to 200°C/Fan 180°C/Gas 6. Prick the pastry base with a fork, line it with greaseproof paper and fill with baking beans, then bake for 20 minutes. Remove the paper and beans and put the pastry back into the oven for another 10 minutes or until the base has cooked but not taken on too much colour. Leave the oven on.

For the filling, trim the leek and split it in half lengthways. Cut it into fine strips, wash these well in cold water, then drain and dry on a cloth. Melt the butter in a wide saucepan, then add the leek and cook gently until tender. Season with a little salt, pepper and the curry powder and continue to cook for 2–3 minutes, then tip everything into a mixing bowl and leave to cool.

Pick through the crabmeat to remove any bones or cartilage and add it to the leek. Whisk the yolks and whole eggs, add the milk and cream and season. Stir the egg mixture into the leek and crab, then pour everything into the pastry base. Gently place the quiche in the oven, still at 200°C/Fan 180°C/Gas 6, and bake for 25 minutes. Sprinkle the grated cheese on top and cook for another 5 minutes or until golden and set. Remove the quiche from the oven and leave to cool a little before cutting it into slices to serve.

To prepare the endive, cut them in half, drizzle with olive oil and season. Heat a ridged grill pan, add the endive and grill until pleasingly charred.

SERVES 8–10

1 medium leek
1 tbsp unsalted butter
1 tbsp Madras curry powder
250g fresh white crabmeat
6 free-range egg yolks
2 free-range eggs
200ml milk
400ml double cream
60g Gruyère cheese, grated
salt
black pepper

SHORTCRUST PASTRY

250g plain flour, sifted, plus
    extra for dusting
120g cold unsalted butter,
    diced
1 free-range egg, beaten
1 tsp salt
2 tbsp cold water

ENDIVE

4 or 5 heads of endive
olive oil

Coquilles Saint-Jacques à la nage et beurre blanc

SCALLOPS WITH VELVET BUTTER SAUCE

It's always best to buy scallops in their shells so you can be sure they are fresh. And ask for diver-caught scallops, not dredged, as the dredging method damages the seabed. This is a beautifully delicate recipe that allows you to appreciate the wonderful flavour of the scallops to the full.

Open the scallops and spoon out the white meat and coral, removing the black stomach and the frill or skirt from each one. Discard the stomachs, but soak the skirts in cold water for 20 minutes, then drain.

Slice the carrot into thin rounds. Cut the onions into thin rings. Trim and wash the celery sticks and cut them into 3cm-long batons.

Pour the wine into a saucepan, add 300ml water and a pinch of salt, then bring to the boil. Add the vegetables and bay leaf and simmer until the vegetables are cooked, then remove them with a slotted spoon. Add the scallop skirts to the liquid and simmer for 15 minutes, then press the liquid through a fine sieve into a bowl.

Pour half the liquid back into the pan and add the cream. Bring it to the boil, then whisk in the butter, a little at a time. Check the seasoning and add a little squeeze of lemon.

Lay the scallops and coral in a wide pan on top of the stove and pour on the other half of the liquid. Bring to a gentle simmer, then cover the scallops with greaseproof paper. After 1 minute, turn the scallops and cook them for a further 2 minutes (depending on their size).

To serve, drain the scallops and place them in warm bowls. Arrange the warm vegetables around them and pour on the hot sauce.

SERVES 4

8 large scallops in their shells
1 medium carrot, peeled
4 large pickling onions, peeled
2 celery sticks
300ml dry white wine
300ml water
1 bay leaf
80ml double cream
100g cold unsalted butter, diced
1 lemon
salt
white pepper

Bouillabaisse Marseillaise

FISH STEW

The name comes from *bouilli* and *baisse* – meaning to
boil, then turn down – because the fish is put into the
pot when boiling and is then slowly poached. As with
many well-loved dishes, there are 101 versions and no
consensus as to which is the ultimate. Traditionally,
whole fish is cooked in the broth and brought to the
table to be filleted and served with the piping hot soup.
My version is a little more dainty, but still remains true
to the original. The weights of the fish given are just a
guide, as what you buy will depend on what's available
on the day. Other fish that can be used are bass, pout,
bream, garfish and grey mullet, but they should be from
the Mediterranean for the recipe to remain authentic.

Scale, gut and fillet the fish – or ask your fishmonger to do this for you. Keep
all the bones for the stock and also keep the mullet livers, if any, to add to
the rouille (see below). Remove any pin bones from the fish and cut them all
into generous portions, keeping any trimmings. Rinse the fish bones well,
put them in a pan and cover with cold water. Bring to the boil, skim, then
cook for 20 minutes to make a fish stock. Pass the stock through a fine sieve.

Heat a tablespoon of olive oil in a huge pan and gently cook the onions, leek,
garlic and chilli until soft. Turn up the heat and add the fish trimmings and
velvet crabs, crushing them down in the pan with a wooden spoon. Cook
over a high heat for 5–6 minutes, then add the saffron, bay, thyme, orange
peel, fennel and tomatoes and mix well. Pour on the pastis, white wine and
enough of the fish stock to cover well, adding a little water if you need it.
Season and simmer for 30 minutes.

Pass the soup through a mouli, then a sieve if necessary, and keep it warm.
Pan-fry the fish in a drizzle of olive oil. Serve the fish with boiled, sliced
potatoes in wide bowls and pour in some hot soup. Serve more soup on the
side and some croutons and rouille.

ROUILLE

Put all the ingredients except the oil in a food processor and blitz to a purée.
With the motor running, slowly add the oil.

SERVES 10

1 x 600g John Dory
500g conger eel
2 x 600g gurnard
2 x 400g rock cod (rascasse)
4 x 500g red mullet
2 x 400g weever
400g monkfish
olive oil
3 onions, chopped
white part of 1 leek, chopped
3 garlic cloves, chopped
1 fresh chilli, chopped
500g velvet crabs
good pinch of saffron strands
2 bay leaves
1 sprig of thyme
peel of 1 small orange
2 sprigs of dried fennel tops
   (or fresh fennel tops)
6 large ripe tomatoes,
   chopped
60ml pastis
500ml white wine
waxy potatoes, boiled and
   sliced, for serving
croutons (see page 339)
salt and black pepper

ROUILLE

2 free-range egg yolks
½ tbsp Dijon mustard
8 garlic cloves, peeled
6 salted anchovy fillets
pinch of saffron, moistened
   with lemon juice
1 red chilli
red mullet livers, pan fried
   (optional)
200ml strong olive oil

Un chef est créatif, mariant des ingrédients comme un poète marie les mots

A cook is creative, marrying ingredients
in the way a poet marries words

ROGER VERGÉ

Aïoli aux légumes, buccins et couteaux

VEGETABLES, WHELKS AND RAZOR CLAMS WITH GARLIC MAYONNAISE

This is Provençal cooking at its best – simple, gutsy food that's meant to be enjoyed outdoors in the sunshine with friends.

To make the aïoli, put the garlic cloves, egg yolks, mustard and lemon juice in a food processor. Blitz while drizzling in the olive oil until the mixture is thick, with the texture of mayonnaise. This can be done in a pestle and mortar, but the food processor does a very good job as long as you don't over-blitz the mixture. Season to taste and set aside.

Wash and trim the courgettes, beans, cauliflower and fennel. Divide the cauliflower into florets and leave the rest of the vegetables whole. Blanch the vegetables separately in boiling, salted water until just cooked, then refresh them in iced water so they stop cooking and keep their vibrant colour. Drain and set aside.

Peel the potatoes and boil in salted water until they are fully cooked. Leave them in the water to keep warm. Boil the whelks in heavily salted water for 20 minutes, then drop in the razor clams and cook for 2–3 minutes more. Drain the whelks and clams well.

Reheat the vegetables in a steamer or in boiling water. Slice them as desired, then arrange on a large platter with the seafood and serve warm, with a bowlful of aïoli.

SERVES 8

400g small courgettes
300g French beans
200g cauliflower
250g baby fennel
500g new potatoes
400g whelks
800g razor clams
salt

AÏOLI

10 garlic cloves, peeled
2 free-range egg yolks
1 tbsp Dijon mustard
juice of 1 lemon
320ml olive oil
salt
black pepper

Calamars farcis au riz sauvage

SQUID STUFFED WITH WILD RICE

This is a classic that just sings with Mediterranean tastes. I like to use lobster stock for its depth of flavour, but at a pinch you could substitute fish stock with a dash of tomato purée. Your fishmonger will clean the squid for you, but ask for them to be kept whole, with the tentacles separate.

Scrub the mussels well, then put them in a large pan with the white wine. Cover and steam the mussels for a few minutes until just done – discard any that haven't opened. Pick out the meat from the shells and set aside. Add the cooking juices from the pan to the lobster stock.

Preheat the oven to 200°C/Fan 180°C/Gas 6. Melt half a tablespoon of the butter in a heavy-based pan that can go in the oven and gently cook the chopped onion and diced peppers until tender. Add the rice and stir until it is all coated with the butter, then pour in 200ml of the lobster stock. Season with the saffron, salt and pepper, then loosely cover with foil and bake in the oven for 20 minutes. Set aside to cool.

When the rice is cool, stir in the egg yolks to bind the stuffing together. Fill the squid with the rice stuffing, carefully pushing it in without damaging the body. Close the opening of each with a wooden cocktail stick. Bring the rest of the lobster stock to a simmer in a wide pan and gently cook the stuffed squid in the stock for 4–5 minutes until tender.

Transfer a few ladlefuls of the liquid to a small pan and boil until reduced to a sauce consistency.

Meanwhile, heat the remaining butter in a pan with the garlic, shallot and parsley. Toss the mussels in the garlicky butter to warm them through. In a separate pan, fry the squid tentacles in a little oil until crispy.

Using a sharp knife, carefully cut the stuffed squid into thick slices and serve with the mussels, fried tentacles and sauce.

SERVES 4

20 mussels

125ml white wine

500ml lobster stock (see page 325)

100g unsalted butter

1 onion, peeled and finely chopped

1 red pepper, deseeded and diced

1 green pepper, deseeded and diced

100g wild rice, soaked overnight in cold water

pinch of saffron strands

2 free-range egg yolks

4 medium squid, cleaned and beaks removed

2 garlic cloves, peeled and finely chopped

1 shallot, peeled and finely chopped

1 small bunch of flatleaf parsley, finely chopped

vegetable oil

salt

black pepper

Moules marinière

MUSSELS IN WHITE WINE

The classic mussel dish – this is quick and simple to make and loved by all. In Normandy they use dry cider instead of white wine and the result is just as delicious. Serve piping hot and provide lots of crusty bread for dipping into the fragrant juices.

Wash and scrub the mussels, discarding any broken ones. Melt the butter in a large pan, then add the onion, celery and garlic and sweat for a few minutes. Pour in the wine and bring to the boil, then add the mussels and cover the pan. Leave for 3 minutes, then shake the pan to toss the mussels around and continue to cook for another 7–8 minutes. All the mussels should have opened by this time, but discard any that haven't.

Remove the mussels with a slotted spoon and put them in a big serving dish or individual bowls. Bring the liquid in the pan back to the boil, then add the crème fraiche, parsley and seasoning. As soon as the liquid has come back to the boil, pour it over the mussels and serve at once.

SERVES 4

3kg mussels
1 tbsp unsalted butter
1 large onion, peeled and finely chopped
4 celery sticks, finely chopped
1 garlic clove, peeled and finely chopped
400ml dry white wine
200g crème fraiche
1 bunch of flatleaf parsley, chopped
salt
black pepper

Truite aux amandes

TROUT WITH ALMONDS

This is best of all cooked with trout you've just caught
yourself but it's always good. Serve with boiled potatoes
and steamed vegetables for mopping up all that butter.

Snip the fins off the trout and remove the guts and gills – or ask your
fishmonger to do this for you. Rinse the fish under cold water and pat them
dry with kitchen paper. Dust them with the seasoned flour.

Heat the oil and half the butter in a frying pan until the butter is frothing.
Add the fish and cook them over a moderate heat for 5 minutes on each side
until golden, while constantly basting them with the butter. Take the pan off
the heat and put the fish on a warm serving dish.

Discard the cooking fat, add the rest of the butter to the pan and heat until
frothy. Add the flaked almonds and toss them in the butter until golden,
then add the lemon juice and pour the contents of the pan over the trout.
Serve at once.

SERVES 4

4 trout, each about 250g
100g plain flour, seasoned
    with salt and black pepper
2 tbsp vegetable oil
120g unsalted butter
60g flaked almonds
juice of 1 lemon

Epigramme de sole

STUFFED SOLE FILLETS

This is a true French classic of Dover sole fillets, stuffed with lobster, sealed in breadcrumbs and fried, then served with a rich lobster sauce. Epigrammes are often made with breast of lamb or veal, but this is a much more luxurious – and expensive – version.

Trim the sole fillets and place them on a piece of cling film. Using the smooth side of a meat mallet or a rolling pin, gently bat the fillets out to double their width. Set them aside with what was the skin side facing up.

Pull the head off the lobster, crack the shell and remove the meat. Cut it into small dice, keeping 4 nice medallions from the tail to garnish the dish.

Heat a tablespoon of oil in a pan and sweat the chopped shallot, celery, carrot and garlic until the shallot is translucent, then add the lobster shell and crush it down with a rolling pin.

Add the brandy, tomato paste, fresh tomato, bay leaf and wine, then boil until the liquid is reduced by half. Add the stock and simmer for 20 minutes, then strain through a fine sieve. Pour the strained liquid back into the pan and reduce again by half. Add 2 tablespoons of this to the diced lobster and set the rest aside. Mix the chopped herbs with the lobster.

Put a generous amount of the lobster stuffing on each sole fillet. Fold over the end of each fillet and tuck it in to make a little parcel enclosing the filling. Spread the flour and breadcrumbs on separate plates and beat the egg in a bowl. Carefully roll each sole parcel in flour, then the beaten egg and finally the breadcrumbs, making sure to seal the edges and keep the shape.

Warm the butter and 2 tablespoons of oil in a frying pan until frothy and foaming. Add the sole parcels and shallow fry them for about 10 minutes, turning them until golden all over and cooked through.

To finish the sauce, add the cream to the reduced lobster stock and boil until it has the consistency of a sauce. Check the seasoning and serve with the fish and some baby turnips and asparagus.

SERVES 4

2 large Dover sole, skinned and filleted (keep the bones for stock)
1 x 500g lobster, cooked
vegetable oil
1 shallot, peeled and chopped
1 celery stick, chopped
½ carrot, peeled and chopped
1 garlic clove, peeled and chopped
2 tbsp brandy
2 tsp tomato paste
1 tomato, cut into quarters
1 bay leaf
100ml dry white wine
400ml fish stock (see page 324)
1 sprig each of tarragon, chervil, chives, chopped
100g plain flour
100g breadcrumbs
1 free-range egg
75g unsalted butter
300ml double cream
salt
black pepper

Filet de sole Véronique

SOLE WITH GREEN GRAPES

This delicate, elegant dish is a real classic of the Escoffier era. Many colleges still use this recipe as a way to teach basic skills and techniques, and it comes up quite often in *Masterchef*. It can be made with most flat fish, such as plaice or lemon sole, but it's best with firm meaty Dover sole. Skinning soles can be tricky so ask your fishmonger to do this for you. They will also fillet the fish if you don't want to do it yourself, but make sure they give you the bones. You can serve this dish very simply with the sauce or go to town with a more elaborate presentation for a special occasion.

SERVES 2

2 x 400g Dover soles, skinned and filleted
1 shallot, peeled and sliced
1 lemon
60ml dry white wine
120g unsalted butter
60ml white vermouth
2 tbsp double cream
1 small bunch of white grapes (preferably Muscat), peeled and deseeded
salt
white pepper

Chop up the bones of the sole and rinse them well. Leave them to soak in cold water for 20 minutes, then drain. To make the stock, put the fish bones in a large saucepan with the sliced shallot, a squeeze of lemon juice and the wine, then pour in cold water to cover. Bring to a gentle boil, skim the surface well and simmer for 20 minutes. Pass the stock through a fine sieve and set aside.

Place the sole fillets on a piece of cling film. Using a rolling pin or a small pan, gently bat the fillets to flatten them out. Roll them up – if you like, you can keep them in place with little wooden skewers.

Preheat the oven to 200°C/Fan 180°C/Gas 6. Put the fillets in a lightly buttered baking dish, season with salt and white pepper, then pour on the stock and vermouth. Cover the fish with some buttered baking parchment and place in the oven to poach gently for 5–6 minutes. Turn the fillets, then put them back in the oven for another 5–6 minutes. When the fish is just cooked, remove it from the oven and pour the cooking liquid into a saucepan. Cover the fish and set it aside to keep warm.

Boil the cooking liquid until it has reduced to a syrup. Add the cream and butter, whisking well until the liquid has emulsified into a creamy sauce.

Serve the sole beautifully garnished with the grapes, a few diced vegetables and a little sauce, with the rest of the sauce in a jug on the side. Alternatively, pour the sauce over the fish before serving and garnish with grapes. Good with some steamed potatoes and green vegetables.

Brandade de morue aux calamars et piment d'Espelette

SALT COD PURÉE WITH CORNISH SQUID AND ESPELETTE PEPPER

Cornish squid doesn't sound very French but it goes beautifully with this classic salt cod purée, which is a brasserie favourite. The brandade is also delicious just as it is with a little toast rubbed with a clove of garlic.

Put the salt cold in a large bowl with a copious amount of fresh water and leave it in the fridge for 48 hours, changing the water at least 4 times.

Cook the potato on a bed of rock salt in a hot oven (220°C/Fan 200°C/Gas 7) until tender, then pass it through a potato ricer and keep warm. Drain the soaked cod and put it in a large saucepan. Pour in the milk to cover and add the bay leaves, thyme and garlic cloves, bruising them first to release their flavour. Bring the milk just up to the boil and then turn off the heat. Leave the fish to rest in the milk for 15 minutes, then carefully flake the flesh, discarding any bones and skin. Set the milk aside.

This next part takes a little skill, as the more olive oil you can emulsify into the brandade the more indulgent the texture will be. Too little oil and the purée will be coarse; too much and it will be an oily mess on the plate.

Start by putting the flaked cod in a food processor with a quarter of its volume of potato. Add a few tablespoons of the poaching milk and start to blend the mixture. Slowly drizzle in the olive oil, as if you were making mayonnaise, until you have a silky smooth mixture. You might need to add a little more milk if the mixture is getting too claggy or more potato if it seems too wet. Season the mixture with white pepper and possibly, although unlikely, a little sea salt. Keep the mixture warm while you cook the squid.

Empty the squid ink into a pan, add a tablespoon of the cod cooking milk and warm it through. Cut the squid bodies into rings and leave the bunches of tentacles whole. Season the squid lightly and cook them briefly on a very hot griddle. Spoon the warm brandade on to hot plates and add some squid and a drizzle of squid ink. Sprinkle with piment d'Espelette and white pepper and add parsley if you like.

You can make the brandade ahead of time and keep it in the fridge. When you're ready to serve, tip it into a pan, add a splash of milk and warm it through gently over a very low heat, making sure it doesn't burn.

SERVES 10 AS A STARTER

400g dried salt cod
1 large baking potato
rock salt
2 litres whole milk
2 bay leaves
1 sprig of thyme
½ head of garlic, cloves
    separated
300ml olive oil
3 sachets of squid ink
500g squid, cleaned
ground piment d'Espelette
    (chilli powder)
coarsely chopped parsley
    (optional)
salt
ground white pepper

Dorade cuite dans sa marinade

BLACK BREAM COOKED IN ITS MARINADE

If you can't get black bream, farmed gilthead bream is
plentiful and works just as well here. This dish can also
be served cold with salad.

Rinse the fish, dry it with kitchen paper and remove any pin bones with
tweezers. Slice the onion into thin rings and the carrot into thin rounds.
Slice the fennel lengthways into thin slices.

To make the marinade, put the wine, water, vinegar, juices, sugar and
cumin seeds in a saucepan, bring to the boil and season with a little salt and
pepper. Add the vegetables and stir, then remove from the heat, cover and
leave to cool completely.

Lay the fish flat in an ovenproof glass or earthenware dish. Pour on the cold
marinade and the olive oil, cover and leave the fish in the fridge to marinate
for 6–12 hours.

Preheat the oven to 190°C/Fan 170°C/Gas 5. Scatter the parsley over the fish,
cover with a piece of greaseproof paper and cook in the oven for 12 minutes.
It should be slightly undercooked and just warm.

SERVES 6

6 fillets of black bream
    (120–150g each)
1 onion, peeled
1 carrot, peeled
1 fennel bulb, trimmed
125ml dry white wine
60ml water
1 tbsp white wine vinegar
juice of ½ orange and
    ½ lemon
1 tsp demerara sugar
½ tsp cumin seeds
3 tbsp strong, fragrant olive
    oil
a few sprigs of flatleaf
    parsley
sea salt
coarsely ground black
    pepper

Tagine de rouget et couscous

TAGINE OF RED MULLET AND COUSCOUS

A tagine is a traditional cooking pot and to be true to
its North African roots, this dish should be cooked in a
tagine – or at least served in one.

Preheat the oven to 220°C/Fan 200°C/Gas 7. Fillet the red mullet, or ask
the fishmonger to do this for you, and remove any pin bones with tweezers.
Cut each fillet in half and place them skin-side up on a lightly oiled baking
sheet. Brush the fish with a little oil and season sparingly with salt.

Put the sultanas in a small saucepan, cover them with cold water and bring
to the boil. Drain and pat dry. Toast the couscous in hot olive oil for about
10 seconds, then pour on about 175ml of boiling water for it to absorb.
Remove the pan from the heat, add a little more oil and fluff the couscous up
with a fork. Add the chopped chilli (with or without seeds, depending on hot
you like your food), spring onions, garlic, sultanas, parsley, lime juice and
season with salt to taste.

Bake the red mullet in the hot oven for a matter of minutes – the skin should
start to blister. Spoon the couscous into hot dishes and place a piece of fish
on top.

If you like, you can add a few thin slices of chorizo on top of the red mullet
before you bake it.

SERVES 8

2 x 500g red mullet
olive oil
1 tbsp sultanas
200g precooked couscous
175ml boiling water
1 red chilli, finely chopped
2 spring onions, sliced
1 garlic clove, peeled and
    finely chopped
a few sprigs of flatleaf parsley
juice of 1 lime
salt

Rouget grillé sur son lit de courgettes

COURGETTE CREAM WITH GRILLED RED MULLET

You might be surprised by the touch of curry here, but there are many French dishes that do include curry powder, especially in the south. This is a really simple recipe, but you need to make the flavoured oil well in advance to give time for the flavours to infuse and develop. The recipe makes far more oil than you need for this dish, but it's a great thing to have in your store cupboard and goes well with salads, fish or grilled chicken. Do give the chargrilled bread a try. It is the ideal accompaniment to the fish, not just a decoration.

First prepare the curry oil. Heat the curry powder carefully in a dry pan for 5 minutes to release the oils and flavour. Add the oil and heat to 40°C, then cover and leave to cool. After 24 hours, pour the oil through a muslin cloth, then store in a bottle in a cool dark place.

Wash and dice all but a couple of the courgettes, slice the onion and crush the garlic cloves.

Melt a tablespoon of butter in a large pan and sweat the vegetables for 5 minutes. Add the 2 teaspoons of curry powder and continue to cook for a further 5 minutes. Pour in the boiling water, season and simmer for 10 minutes, then add the basil leaves and blitz in a food processor until smooth. Keep the mixture warm until you are ready to serve.

Cut the remaining courgettes into thin ribbons on a mandolin or into fine strips. Cook these gently in a little butter for a minute or so, then season and keep warm. Brush the slices of bread with oil and grill them on a hot ridged grill pan until toasted and nicely marked with the grill lines.

Check that all the pin bones have been removed from the red mullet fillets, then season them lightly and smear them with olive oil. Heat the grill pan and cook the mullet until just tender.

Serve a bed of courgette cream on to each plate and add some ribbons, or strips, of courgette. Place the fish on top and drizzle with the curry-infused olive oil. Serve with the slices of grilled bread.

SERVES 4

600g courgettes
1 white onion, peeled
2 garlic cloves, peeled
unsalted butter
2 tsp Madras curry powder
800ml boiling water
handful of basil leaves
4 slices of sourdough bread
olive oil
4 small red mullet (200–300g each), filleted but with skin on
salt
black pepper

CURRY OIL

3 tbsp Madras curry powder
1 litre olive oil

Le bon repas est celui qui est aussi agréable à la degustation qu'à la digestion

A good meal should be as pleasing to the taste as to the digestion

Pôchouse Bourguignonne

BURGUNDIAN FRESHWATER FISH STEW

This classic stew is made with fish native to the rivers of Burgundy. Traditionally, there should be some rich oily fish, like salmon, while the rest can be white fish, such as pike, perch, tench or carp. Some people worry about eating freshwater species but I think if you use fish from sustainable sources it's fine. The dish is finished with the traditional Burgundian garnish of mushrooms and glazed onions.

Clean and fillet all the fish, keeping the bones, or ask your fishmonger to do this for you. Cut the fish into manageable pieces, bearing in mind that this is a soupy dish and is eaten with a spoon, so the portions shouldn't be too large. Blanch the ventrèche in boiling water for 5 minutes, then cut it into lardons, keeping any trimmings and end bits for the soup. Gently fry the lardons with a little drop of oil and set them aside for later. Slice the mushrooms, keeping any trimmings.

Warm a tablepoon of oil in a pan and gently cook the sliced onion with the mushroom and ventrèche trimmings until lightly coloured. Add the fish bones and trimmings, deglaze the pan with the brandy, then pour in the wine and add the bouquet garni. Add water to cover, season with salt and pepper, then simmer for 20 minutes.

Meanwhile, prepare the garnish. Melt a knob of butter in a pan, add the button onions and sweat until lightly coloured. Add a couple of spoonfuls of the soup and cover with a piece of greaseproof paper until cooked. Sauté the mushrooms in butter until cooked and coloured.

To prepare the croutons, cut some thin slices of baguette, brush with oil and rub with a cut clove of garlic. Place them on a baking sheet and bake in a preheated oven at 200°C/Fan 180°C/Gas 6 for 10 minutes or until crispy.

Blitz the soup and press it through a fine sieve, then add a tablespoon of butter to shine and enrich the sauce.

Heat a tablespoon each of oil and butter in a frying pan and fry the fish until just cooked. Arrange the portions in soup plates and garnish with the ventrèche lardons, mushrooms and button onions. Then pour in the soup and add a baguette crouton. Sprinkle with parsley and serve at once.

SERVES 4

1 small pike (or a 300g fillet)
1 small trout
2 perch
2 x 200g pieces of salmon
200g smoked ventrèche (see page 343)
vegetable oil
12 button mushrooms, wiped
1 onion, peeled and sliced
good slosh of brandy (about 2 tbsp)
375ml Chablis or good white Chardonnay
1 bouquet garni, made up of leek, parsley stalks, bay leaves, thyme and celery (see page 342)
unsalted butter
10 button onions, peeled
1 baguette
2 garlic cloves
chopped flatleaf parsley
salt
black pepper

Aile de raie au beurre noir

SKATE WITH BLACK BUTTER

The butter in this classic fish dish is not actually black but *noisette* – nut brown – and it's important to use good-quality butter as it really does make a difference. With thick skate wings, it is best to poach them gently first, but small thin skate wings can be cooked *à la meunière* – dredged with flour and fried – and then you can add the black butter sauce afterwards. My preference is to have a thick meaty piece of skate served on the bone.

Put the onion in a large pan with the chopped celery, vinegar, wine, peppercorns and bay leaf. Add the water and a generous pinch of salt, then bring to a simmer for 10 minutes. Allow the liquid to cool slightly, then put in the skate. Bring the water back to a simmer, then turn off the heat and leave until the skate is cool enough to handle. This should be enough to cook the skate.

Melt the butter in a separate pan, then turn up the heat and cook until golden brown – don't let it burn. Add the capers with a little of their pickling vinegar, the chopped lemon segment and the parsley, if using. Remove the skate from the cooking liquid, drain well and put it in the warm pan with the butter and capers for 30 seconds. Serve at once.

SERVES 2

1 onion, peeled and
    quartered
1 celery stick, chopped
1 tbsp white wine vinegar
100ml white wine
6 black peppercorns
1 bay leaf
1 litre water
2 x 200g pieces of skate,
    skinned
80g good-quality unsalted
    butter
1 tbsp capers in vinegar
1 lemon segment, chopped
1 tbsp chopped flatleaf
    parsley (optional)
salt

Some of the most famous of all French classics feature
chicken, duck and other birds. Always buy the best-
quality poultry you can afford, as these dishes should
be a treat, lovingly prepared and richly enjoyed.
There's no point working with second-rate birds.
Guinea fowl has a stronger flavour than chicken
and is a good introduction to feathered game, then
I would urge you to get more adventurous and try
others. Always keep the bones and wings of poultry
to make a flavoursome stock.

Poulets, canards et gibiers à plume

Poulet sauté Marengo

CHICKEN WITH CRAYFISH AND FRIED EGGS

Legend has it that this dish was created for Napoleon after the battle of Marengo on 14 June 1800. I love the idea that his chef scoured the vicinity for ingredients and came up with a feast fit for the Emperor. It's always good to cook meat on the bone, as it retains its shape, flavour and moisture, and this recipe is no exception.

Cut the chicken into 8 pieces. Keep the breasts on the bone and cut each of them in half, leaving the wings on. Section the legs into drumstick and thigh. Preheat the oven to 180°C/Fan 160°/Gas 4.

Dust the chicken pieces in the seasoned flour, then pan fry them in a little oil until brown all over. Remove the chicken and set aside. Discard the oil from the pan, add a tablespoon of fresh oil and sweat the chopped onion until tender and just starting to colour. Add the garlic and wine, then simmer for 2–3 minutes, stirring to lift any sticky bits from the base of the pan. Tip everything into an ovenproof pan with the chicken, bouquet garni, tomatoes and stock or water. Bring to a gentle simmer, cover with a piece of greaseproof paper and place in the oven for 40 minutes.

Take the pan out of the oven, remove the chicken and pour the cooking liquid through a fine sieve into a saucepan, pressing well. Bring the liquid to the boil, add the crayfish and mushrooms and continue to simmer until they are cooked and the sauce has reached the consistency of single cream.

Meanwhile, crack the eggs into individual cups. Heat the vegetable oil to 160°C in a deep-fat fryer, then gently tip the eggs into the oil. Cook for 4–5 minutes, depending on size – the eggs should have runny yolks and crisp, slightly coloured whites. Drain them on kitchen paper to remove the excess oil. Quickly fry the cubes of baguette in the oil to make croutons and drain them on kitchen paper.

Pour the sauce back into the cooking pan or a warm serving dish with the chicken. Add the croutons and deep-fried eggs, sprinkle with chopped parsley and bring to the table to serve.

SERVES 4

1 free-range chicken
flour, seasoned with salt and pepper
vegetable oil
1 large onion, peeled and chopped
2 garlic cloves, peeled and crushed
250ml dry white wine
1 bouquet garni, made up of bay leaves, thyme and parsley stalks (see page 342)
6 large tomatoes, peeled, deseeded and chopped
250ml chicken stock (see page 320) or water
12 whole crayfish
12 button mushrooms
4 free-range eggs
stale baguette, cut into cubes
handful of chopped flatleaf parsley
salt
black pepper

Poulet rôti en cocotte Dijonnaise

POT-ROAST CHICKEN WITH MUSTARD

Dijon is famed for its mustard, hence the title of this wonderfully simple and delicious chicken recipe. In fact, I like to use several different mustards here, as each adds its own character and flavour to the finished dish. It's always worth having a selection of mustards anyway and they keep well. Savora mustard contains a number of spices and a touch of honey sweetness.

Preheat the oven to 200°C/Fan 180°C/Gas 6. Melt the butter and oil in a roasting pot or flameproof casserole dish on the hob. Season the chicken, then add it to the pot and colour it on all sides.

Put the chicken in the oven to roast for 1¼ hours, but every 15 minutes turn the bird, baste it and add some white wine until you've used up all the wine. Once the chicken is cooked, take it out of the pot and set it aside to rest.

Slice the mushrooms, add them to the pot and cook them for 2–3 minutes. Pour in the brandy and flambé briefly, then set aside to keep warm.

For the sauce, melt the butter in a heavy-based pan, add the flour and cook for 3 minutes. Pour in the milk, whisking well, bring to the boil and cook for 7–8 minutes. Stir in the crème fraiche, then take the pan off the heat and whisk in the mustards and tarragon. Add the mushrooms and any liquid from the roasting pot to the sauce. Do not boil the sauce again or it may split and taste bitter.

Joint or carve the chicken and serve with the mushroom sauce. You need nothing more than a few vegetables and a twirl of noodles.

SERVES 2–4

50g unsalted butter
2 tbsp vegetable oil
1 x 1.6kg free-range chicken
200ml dry white wine
300g button mushrooms, wiped
100ml Cognac
salt
black pepper

SAUCE

1 tbsp unsalted butter
1 tbsp flour
500ml milk
200ml crème fraiche
2 tbsp grain mustard
2 tbsp strong Dijon mustard
2 tbsp Savora mustard
1 bunch of fresh tarragon, finely chopped

Poulet Dauphinois

CHICKEN WITH FRESH WALNUTS

The sauce for this delicious chicken dish tastes beautifully creamy but is actually thickened with walnuts. It's best made with fresh 'wet' walnuts, which are available for just a few weeks in autumn. These are walnuts that have just been picked so the insides are still damp and juicy, with a wonderful mild flavour.

Pour 3 litres of water into a large pan and add the roughly chopped vegetables, garlic, thyme, bay leaf and a good pinch of salt. Simmer for 20 minutes, then leave to cool until tepid.

Add the chicken to the pan and bring everything to a very gentle simmer. Cook for 1½ hours, keeping the water at a slow gentle simmer – it mustn't boil – and topping up with extra water if necessary. Once the chicken is cooked, take it out, remove the skin and cut the flesh into large bite-sized pieces. Cover them with a damp cloth and keep warm.

Add the chicken bones to the cooking stock, bring it to the boil and simmer for a further 20 minutes, skimming off any fat and scum. Pass this through a fine sieve. Shell the fresh walnuts.

Pour 300ml of the sieved stock into a blender, add the shelled fresh walnuts and blitz to a smooth creamy sauce. Season with salt, pepper and a hint of grated nutmeg. Pour the sauce over the chicken pieces and serve warm, garnished with toasted walnut halves, deep-fried parsley and a drizzle of walnut oil.

GARNISH

To deep-fry the parsley, pick the leaves from the stems, wash and dry well. Heat some vegetable oil in a pan, add the leaves and fry for a few seconds, then drain on kitchen paper. Put the walnut halves in a pan with a drop of vegetable oil and toast them in a frying pan on the hob.

SERVES 4

3 litres water
1 carrot, peeled and roughly chopped
½ leek, roughly chopped
1 onion, peeled and roughly chopped
3 garlic cloves, peeled and chopped
1 sprig of thyme
1 bay leaf
1 x 1.4kg free-range chicken
300g fresh wet walnuts
freshly grated nutmeg
salt
black pepper

GARNISH
bunch of curly parsley
vegetable oil, for frying
12 dried walnut halves
2 tbsp walnut oil

Poulet de Bresse en vessie

BRESSE CHICKEN COOKED IN A PIG'S BLADDER

Bresse is just north of Lyon and famous for its chickens, which are expensive but so good and deserve special treatment. This dish is a great classic of French cuisine and one that I first came across when working for Alain Chapel at Mionnay. On a busy night we would sell 20 of these chickens and the wonderful aroma filled the kitchen and dining room alike. Cooking in a pig's bladder like this is a method that cooks have used for centuries, and the current fashion for cooking meat in vacuum pouches in a water bath is simply a version of this – it's nothing new.

Pigs' bladders are sold dried so your *vessie* will need to be soaked in cold water for a couple of hours until soft and pliable.

Remove the giblets from the chicken. Trim the neck, winglets and feet and set them aside with the giblets. Now put a little oil on your fingers and slide slices of truffle under the skin of the chicken breast, being very careful not to break the skin. Season the inside of the chicken well, then place it inside the bladder. Add more seasoning, then pour the stock, brandy, Madeira and truffle juice into the bladder with the chicken. Knot the top and tie it with string to be on the safe side, then place it in a large pan of simmering, salted water to cook for 1½ hours. Leave to rest for 15 minutes before serving.

While the chicken is poaching, blanch the vegetables separately in salted, boiling water, keeping them al dente, then refresh them in cold water and set aside. Trim the girolles so they're ready to cook at the last minute.

Heat the vegetable oil in a pan and brown the chicken trimmings, giblets and shallots, then deglaze with Madeira. Add the stock, bring it to a simmer and cook for 15 minutes. Pass the liquid through a fine sieve, then pour it back into the pan, add the cream and reduce to a sauce consistency. Keep the sauce warm.

Cook the girolles in a little butter and season with salt and pepper. Warm the blanched vegetables through in butter.

Once the chicken has rested, break open the bladder and carve the bird. Serve with the sauce, vegetables and girolles.

SERVES 4

1 pig's bladder (*vessie*)
1 x 1.6kg Bresse chicken
olive oil
1 truffle, cooked and thinly
    sliced
1 tbsp each of chicken stock
    (see page 320), Madeira
    wine and brandy
1 tbsp truffle juice (available
    in cans)
salt
black pepper

GARNISH AND SAUCE
baby leeks, carrots, turnips,
    mooli (white radish),
    mangetout
handful of girolle
    mushrooms, if available,
    or other wild mushrooms
1 tbsp vegetable oil
2 shallots, peeled and
    chopped
2 tbsp Madeira wine
400ml chicken stock
300ml double cream
unsalted butter, for frying

Suprême de volaille Agnès Sorel

POACHED CHICKEN AGNÈS SOREL

This classic recipe of poached chicken with chicken mousse and a supreme sauce was created by the great French chef Auguste Escoffier (1846–1935). He made it in honour of Agnès Sorel, mistress of King Charles VII of France and a keen cook herself.

Heat a knob of butter in a frying pan and add all the mushrooms. Season and add a squeeze of lemon juice to keep the mushrooms white, then cook them until tender. Remove them from the pan and set aside to cool.

Take one of the chicken supremes and blitz it with the egg white in a food processor until smooth. Pass it through a fine sieve to remove any sinew or gristle. Beat in about 250ml of the cream to make a mousse that's light but still holds its shape. It should have the texture of a thick mayonnaise.

Preheat the oven to 180°C/Fan 160°C/Gas 4. Butter 2 small ramekins measuring about 3cm across and 4cm high. Finely slice the small mushrooms and use them to line the ramekins, then fill them with the chicken mousse. Cover the ramekins with foil and place them in a bain-marie – a small roasting tin will do fine. Add boiling water to about half way up the sides of the moulds and cook them for about 10 minutes, depending on the size. The mousse should feel firm to the touch when done. Keep them warm in the tin of hot water until needed.

Pour the stock into a pan and add the herbs and seasoning. Gently poach the remaining chicken for 15–20 minutes until cooked through. Keep the stock at a simmer and do not allow it to boil. Remove the chicken and keep it warm while you make the sauce. Set aside the cooking stock for the sauce.

Put the chopped shallots and mushroom trimmings in a saucepan with the wine and cook until the liquid has reduced and the pan is almost dry. Pour in half the chicken cooking stock and reduce by half, then add the remaining cream and reduce again. Meanwhile, pour the veal jus into a separate pan and boil to reduce it to a sticky glaze. Cut the ox tongue into thin rounds and finely slice the large mushrooms.

To serve, slice each chicken supreme into 3 pieces and put them on warm plates. Place some slices of ox tongue and mushroom on top and brush them with the veal glaze. Turn out a chicken mousse on to each plate and serve with the sauce. Add some deep-fried salsify crisps if you like (see page 338).

SERVES 2

unsalted butter
6 large white mushrooms, trimmed and wiped
10 button mushrooms, trimmed and wiped
1 lemon
3 boneless free-range chicken supremes, trimmed and skin removed
1 free-range egg white
500ml double cream
500ml chicken stock
a few sprigs of thyme
1 bay leaf
2 shallots, peeled and chopped
250ml dry white wine
200ml veal jus (see page 329)
100g cooked ox tongue
salt
black pepper

Poulet de Bresse aux langoustines

BRESSE CHICKEN WITH LANGOUSTINES

The combination of chicken and langoustines may seem odd, but I think this is truly delicious and it was a great favourite on the menu at Le Gavroche for many years. The dish is made extra special by using a wonderful Bresse chicken if you can find one.

SERVES 4

1 Bresse chicken (1.3–1.5kg)
2 tbsp olive oil
50g unsalted butter
16 langoustines
1 onion, peeled and chopped
100ml Madeira wine
250ml chicken stock
    (see page 320)
4 ripe tomatoes, peeled,
    deseeded and diced
700ml double cream
1 black truffle (optional)
salt
black pepper

Joint the chicken into breasts, legs and thighs and season with salt and pepper. Heat the olive oil with the butter in a sauté pan until foaming, then add the chicken. Cook for 15 minutes, turning twice, until golden and cooked through.

Cook the langoustines in salted, boiling water for 2 minutes or less, depending on their size. Drain and cool, then remove the heads and shell the tails, reserving the shells.

Remove the chicken from the pan and keep it warm. Tip out half the cooking fat, add the onion to the pan and cook until lightly browned. Add the langoustine heads and shells and crush them with a wooden spoon, keeping the pan over a low heat. Deglaze the pan with the Madeira, then add the stock and tomatoes and cook until the pan is nearly dry. Add the cream, bring to the boil and reduce to a light sauce consistency. Pass through a fine sieve into a clean pan.

Reheat the chicken and langoustine tails in the sauce, taking care not to let it boil or the langoustines will toughen. Serve immediately with fresh pasta if you like. Garnish with a sliced, cooked truffle for an extra treat.

Poulet aux lactaires délicieux et rhum

CHICKEN WITH SAFFRON MILK-CAP MUSHROOMS AND DARK RUM

Saffron milk-cap mushrooms can be found in pine forests in autumn. They're not good to eat raw as they have a bitter taste, but this disappears when they are cooked. Check them over for any grit and pine needles, then trim them with a knife.

Season the chicken supremes. Heat a little oil and half the butter in a thick-based pan and cook the chicken, skin-side down, over a medium to high heat until the skin is golden. Lower the heat and turn the chicken over to cook on the other side.

Plunge the mushrooms into salted, boiling water for 1 minute, then drain in a colander and pat dry with a cloth. Cut them into small pieces.

When the chicken is cooked, remove it from the pan and trim the wing tips. Discard the fat from the pan, then add the remaining butter and cook the mushrooms and shallots until golden brown. Pour in the rum, boil for 1 minute, then add the crème fraiche and check the seasoning. Boil for 2 minutes, then serve immediately with the chicken breasts.

A word of warning – never eat wild mushrooms that you have gathered without being absolutely sure what they are and that they are edible.

SERVES 6

6 free-range chicken supremes, with wing tips and skin
vegetable oil
80g butter
450g saffron milk-cap mushrooms
4 shallots, peeled and finely sliced
75ml good-quality dark rum
180ml crème fraiche
salt
black pepper

Baton royal

STUFFED BUTTER ROLLS

Real extravagance in terms of work, ingredients and satisfaction, this recipe dates back to the late 1800s. It is very good to eat and one of my father's great favourites. The filling can be fish, meat or vegetable, but the batons must be served immediately or the breadcrumb coating may become soggy.

First make the filling. Sweat the shallot in a little butter, then add the chicken supremes, season well and add the truffle juice, chicken stock and bay leaf. Simmer gently until the supremes are cooked, turning them after 4 minutes. Take the chicken out and set aside, then reduce the poaching liquid over a high heat. Once it's become almost a glaze, add the cream and bring to the boil, then pass the sauce through a fine sieve. Dice the chicken and fold it into the cream sauce.

Check that the rolls of butter are really cold. Cut them in half and roll them in flour, then beaten egg and finally the seasoned breadcrumbs, pressing a little to ensure a good coating.

Heat the clarified butter and the dripping or lard to 140°C in a deep-fat fryer. Add the coated butter cylinders and fry them for about 7–8 minutes so the interior is as golden as the exterior. Remove them from the fat and leave to drain and cool for a few minutes, then carefully cut the top off each baton and pour out any hot melted butter.

Stuff the batons with the filling and top each one with some diced truffle before serving.

SERVES 4 AS A STARTER

FILLING
1 shallot, peeled and sliced
unsalted butter
2 free-range chicken supremes, skin removed
50ml truffle juice (available in cans)
500ml chicken stock (see page 320)
1 bay leaf
120ml double cream
60g cooked black truffle, diced
salt
black pepper

BATONS
2 x 250g cylinders of unsalted butter (fridge cold)
4 tbsp flour
2 free-range eggs, beaten
400g white breadcrumbs, seasoned with salt and pepper
1kg clarified butter (see page 330) or ghee
1kg clarified dripping or frying lard

Crêtes de coq demidoff

CRUMBED COCKSCOMBS WITH TRUFFLE

In France, chickens are usually sold whole, with the head, and we like to use every part. Nothing goes to waste. If you can get hold of some cockscombs, try this and you'll be surprised how good they taste.

Wash the cockscombs and pull out any remaining feathers. Put them in a pan with salted water, add a little lemon juice and bring to the boil. Simmer until the cockscombs are tender and easy to pierce with the point of a knife – this will probably take about an hour and a half or so depending on how big they are. Leave the cockscombs to cool in the water, then remove them and pat them dry.

Meanwhile, make the stuffing. Heat the duck fat in a pan and fry the chicken livers until pink, adding the shallots, seasoning and a splash of brandy. Leave to cool, then chop the mixture to make a coarse paste and add the chopped truffle.

Using a sharp knife, carefully open up each cockscomb from the base to make a pocket and fill the pockets with the stuffing. Heat the oil to 180°C in a large pan or deep-fat fryer.

Spread the flour and breadcrumbs on separate plates and beat the eggs in a bowl. Dust the stuffed cockscombs with flour, then dip them in the egg and lastly the breadcrumbs. Deep-fry them in batches until crisp, watching out as the oil may spit, then drain them on a cloth.

Serve with some deep-fried parsley (see page 136) and a bowl of Béarnaise sauce (see page 331).

SERVES 4 AS A STARTER

350g cockscombs
1 lemon
1 tbsp duck fat
125g free-range chicken
    livers
2 shallots, peeled and
    chopped
brandy
1 small truffle, chopped
vegetable oil, for frying
4 tbsp flour
6 tbsp breadcrumbs
2 free-range eggs
1 big bunch of curly parsley
salt
black pepper

Caneton Gavroche 67–89

ROAST DUCK, CRISPY LEGS AND WARM LIVER PURÉE

Rich and delicious, this is one of the first duck dishes to
appear on the menu at Le Gavroche. The duck is served
two ways – first the breast, very rare and tender, and
then the well-cooked duck legs.

Peel the carrot and turnips, then trim and turn them into 2 small barrel
shapes (see page 343) per person. Julienne the rest – keep the trimmings.
Cook the barrels in a small pan with a tablespoon of butter and a little water
and salt until tender and glazed, then set aside. Cook the julienne vegetables
in another tablespoon of butter and 4 tablespoons of the duck stock. Season
and cook until the vegetables are glazed and the liquid is reduced by half.

Preheat the oven to 220°C/Fan 200°C/Gas 7. Heat a little oil in a roasting pan
on the hob, season the duck cavity, then colour the duck on all sides. Add the
vegetable trimmings, a roughly chopped shallot and the duck winglets. Place
the pan in the preheated oven with the duck breast-side up and roast for
20 minutes. Remove and put the duck on a rack breast-side down so that the
juices flow into the breast. Leave to rest for 10 minutes.

Add a good drop of vegetable oil to a very hot frying pan and add the cleaned
and trimmed liver, the foie gras and the remaining chopped shallot. Season
well and cook for about 2 minutes – the livers should still be very pink.
Immediately place them all on a drum sieve and press through, adding the fat
and juices that have run from the roast duck. Collect the purée in a small pan
and whisk well with a little of the duck stock to make a thick creamy sauce.
Warm gently before serving, but do not overheat or it will go grainy.

Put the roasting pan back on the hob and heat to caramelise the contents.
Add the port and the rest of the stock , then simmer for 10 minutes. Pass the
sauce through a fine sieve, then pour it back into the pan and reduce to the
desired consistency. Whisk in the remaining tablespoon of cold butter.

Remove the legs from the duck, place them in a pan skin-side up and roast
in a preheated oven, at 220°C/Fan 200°C/Gas 7, for about 15 minutes or until
well done and crispy. Remove the breasts from the carcass and peel off the
skin. Trim off any sinew and fat, then cut each breast diagonally into 5 slices,
keeping the shape of the breast. Place the duck on a hot plate and spoon over
the liver purée. Serve with the hot vegetables and sauce, then bring out the
hot crispy legs and serve on a bed of watercress and a little duck sauce.

SERVES 2

1 large carrot
2 large turnips
3 tbsp unsalted butter
600ml duck stock
   (see page 322)
vegetable oil
1 Challans duck (or any
   good-quality free-range
   duck), wishbone and
   winglets removed and
   set aside
2 shallots, peeled
100g duck liver
40g raw foie gras
160ml port
2 bunches of watercress
salt
black pepper

Caneton Gavroche en pot-au-feu

POACHED DUCK WITH STUFFED CABBAGE

Challans ducks are from the Vendée area of France and are well known for their wonderful flavour and tender flesh, but you can use any good-quality duck. This is a much-loved dish at Le Gavroche and an adaptation of the richer version that was on the menu in the seventies and eighties (opposite). The new recipe, with the meat served with delicate vegetables and a light consommé, has echoes of Asian cookery and is light and fragrant.

Peel the turnips and carrots, then trim and turn them into large barrel shapes (see page 343). Wash the leeks and trim the white parts into 4 pieces the same size as the turnips. Set the prepared vegetables aside for later and keep all the trimmings.

Remove the wishbone and winglets from the duck and season the cavity. Wrap the duck up tightly in a tea towel or muslin cloth, then tie it tightly with string – like a parcel.

Place the duck in a deep pot with all the vegetable trimmings, the celery, herbs, garlic and spices, then add the stock and just enough water to cover by 5cm. Season with salt and bring to a simmer, then turn the heat down to barely a tremble. It's very important to keep the liquid at simmering point because the stock will then remain clear. If you allow the stock to boil it will become murky. Turn the duck 2 or 3 times, skim the surface well and leave to cook for 1 hour and 45 minutes. When the cooking time is up, leave the duck to cool in the liquid until hand hot – this should take about 45 minutes.

Carefully remove the duck. The stock should be clear and should not need clarifying – just pass it gently through a fine sieve. Ladle some of the stock into a clean pan, bring it to a simmer and add the turnips, carrots and leeks that you prepared earlier.

Carve the duck which should be so tender you can spoon it off the bones. Serve the meat, white and dark, in deep bowls with the vegetables and stuffed cabbage (see overleaf), then ladle in some stock, sprinkled with a little tarragon and chervil. I also serve this with sauce Albert and pear chutney (see overleaf) on the side.

SERVES 4

4 large turnips

4 carrots

2 leeks

1 large Challans duck
    (about 2.5kg)

½ head of celery, chopped

1 sprig of thyme

2 bay leaves

2 garlic cloves

6 star anise

2 cloves

1 tbsp black pepper, plus
    extra for seasoning

chopped tarragon and
    chervil, for garnish

1 litre chicken stock
    (see page 320)

salt

STUFFED CABBAGE

Blanch the cabbage leaves in salted, boiling water, then drain them and refresh them in cold water. Blitz the chicken breast and egg white together in a food processor, then press the mixture through a fine sieve. Tip the mixture into a bowl set over ice, beat in the cream and season with salt and pepper. Fold in the diced foie gras and herbs.

Divide the mixture between the 4 blanched cabbage leaves and wrap them in cling film, trimming off any excess leaf. Steam the stuffed leaves over a pan of simmering water for 8–10 minutes until cooked through, then remove the cling film before serving.

SAUCE ALBERT

Put the horseradish and stock in a saucepan and simmer for 10 minutes, then add the cream and cook for a further 5 minutes. If you prefer a smooth sauce, pass it through a fine sieve. Add the crumbs and seasoning, simmer for 5 minutes until dissolved and creamy in consistency. Mix the egg yolk with the mustard and then whisk this into the sauce.

PEAR CHUTNEY

Put the sugar in a large, thick-based, non-aluminium saucepan and add the apple, onion, orange rind, juice, salt, ginger, spices and vinegar. Simmer for about 30 minutes, stirring frequently, until thick and syrupy.

Meanwhile, peel, core and roughly chop the pears. Blanch the tomatoes in boiling water for 15 seconds, then refresh them in ice-cold water. Peel the tomatoes, cut them in half and remove the seeds, then chop the tomato flesh. Add the pears, tomatoes and sultanas to the saucepan and simmer until the pears are tender.

Pour the chutney into sterilised glass jars and seal while hot. Store in a cool, dark place or in the fridge for up to 6 months. If you are planning to make the duck dish it's best to prepare the chutney at least a few days ahead if you can. It's a great chutney to have in your kitchen and it goes well with all kinds of boiled meats.

STUFFED CABBAGE

4 tender green leaves
  of savoy cabbage
½ free-range chicken
  breast, skinless and
  boneless
1 egg white
200ml double cream
80g cooked foie gras, diced
2 tbsp chopped chives and
  parsley
salt
black pepper

SAUCE ALBERT

100g freshly grated
  horseradish
200ml chicken stock
300ml double cream
60g fresh white
  breadcrumbs
1 free-range egg yolk
1 tbsp English mustard
salt
black pepper

PEAR CHUTNEY

300g caster sugar
120g grated peeled Bramley
  apple
120g onion, peeled and
  chopped
1 tbsp coarsely grated orange
  rind
juice of 2 oranges
½ tbsp salt
60g root ginger, chopped
½ tsp ground cinnamon
1 tsp grated nutmeg
1 tsp cayenne pepper
2 pinches of saffron strands
300ml white wine vinegar
750g pears
250g tomatoes
80g sultanas

Charlotte au confit de canard

BREAD CHARLOTTE WITH CONFIT DUCK

This is a Roux Christmas favourite and never fails to
please. Jars of duck confit with hearts and gizzards are
now fairly easy to find, but if you're squeamish you can
leave out the offal and add extra duck legs instead. You
can make this in individual moulds or in one large tin.

Cut the bread into medium slices and remove the crusts, then cut the slices
in half again. Moisten the bread with some of the duck fat from the drained
confit – melt the fat and brush it on, or dip the bread into it. Line the
moulds with bread, making sure that the slices overlap so there are no gaps
and that they are well pressed into the moulds.

Sweat the shallots in a pan with a little duck fat and cook until soft. Add the
port and reduce by half, then add the stock and reduce again until the sauce
has reduced to a syrupy consistency and is thick enough to coat the back of a
spoon. Leave the sauce to cool.

Trim the mushrooms and sear them in a frying pan with a knob of duck fat.
Add the chopped garlic and parsley, cook for a few minutes longer, then tip
the contents of the pan into a bowl and set aside to cool.

Remove the skin from the duck legs and flake the meat. Slice the gizzards
and hearts. Add all the meat to the mushrooms with just enough of the sticky
port sauce to bind. Season with a generous amount of pepper. Preheat the
oven to 200°C/Fan 180°C/Gas 6.

Divide the mixture between the bread-lined moulds and cover the tops
with foil. Bake for 20 minutes. Leave to rest for 10 minutes before turning
the charlottes out of the moulds, then serve with the remaining port sauce,
warmed through, and some extra wild mushrooms if you like – cook these in
a little duck fat.

If you prefer to make one large charlotte, use a round cake tin, measuring
about 20cm in diameter by 10cm deep, with a removable base. Cook the
charlotte for 35–40 minutes and leave to rest as above.

SERVES 6 AS A MAIN COURSE

1 large loaf of good-quality
bread
duck fat from the confit
4 shallots, peeled and
chopped
200ml port
750ml veal stock
300g mixed wild
mushrooms, wiped
2 garlic cloves, peeled and
chopped
2 tbsp chopped flatleaf
parsley
6 confit duck legs
6 confit gizzards
6 confit hearts (optional)
black pepper

*La meilleure cuisson est celle
qui prend en considération les
produits de la saison*

The best cooking is that which takes into
consideration the products of the season
AUGUSTE ESCOFFIER

Magret de canard Bordelaise

DUCK BREAST WITH RED WINE SAUCE

This recipe should be made with a fattened duck breast, which is large enough to feed two people. If you can't find one of these, use two normal duck breasts instead. The Bordelaise garnish of bone marrow is an essential part of this rich dish, along with the red wine and shallot sauce.

Trim the duck breast, then score the skin. Place the breast in a warm pan, skin-side down, season and cook gently to render the fat and crisp the skin. The breast will take about 12 minutes for pink meat, but only cook it on the flesh side for a couple of minutes. Leave it to rest before carving.

Put the sliced shallots in a pan with the wine and sugar. Bring to the boil, then add the herb bundle. Cook until the liquid has almost completely reduced, then add the stock and continue to reduce until it has the consistency of a sauce. Remove the herbs, then stir in the butter and seasoning to finish the sauce.

Simmer the bone marrow in salted water for 5–6 minutes, then drain. Place some bone marrow on the sliced duck and serve with the sauce and wild mushrooms. Lovely with some little potato cakes too – see the recipe for pommes Macaire on page 174.

WILD MUSHROOMS

Trim and wash the mushrooms as necessary. Heat a little vegetable oil in a pan and fry the mushrooms for 2 minutes. Drain, tipping away any water, then put the mushrooms back in the pan with the butter, chopped shallot and garlic. Season and finish with chopped parsley.

SERVES 2

1 fattened duck breast
4 large shallots, peeled and sliced
300ml red wine
1 tbsp caster sugar
bouquet garni, made up of a thyme, bay leaf and parsley (see page 342)
500ml good veal stock
1 tbsp unsalted butter
100g beef bone marrow (removed from the bone)
salt
black pepper

WILD MUSHROOMS

160g mixed wild mushrooms
1 tbsp unsalted butter
1 shallot, peeled and chopped
1 garlic clove, peeled and chopped
1 bunch of flatleaf parsley, chopped

Salmis de bécasse

SALMI OF WOODCOCK

A salmi can be made with all kinds of game, but
invariably has a rich wine-based sauce. This is
thickened with liver, or sometimes blood, and has
a depth of flavour that salmi aficionados appreciate.
In this recipe, the woodcock are roasted complete with
guts, as is the tradition. The birds are then drawn and
any inedible parts such as the gizzard removed. In a
classic salmi the meats are reheated in the sauce, but
I find that this overcooks the game and spoils the dish.

Season the woodcock. Heat the oil and a tablespoon of the butter in a
large pan on the hob and roast the woodcock for 8–10 minutes. Remove
the breasts and legs from the woodcock and keep them warm. Set the
heads aside.

Remove the intestines from the birds, discarding the gizzards, and chop
them finely. Put them in a bowl and beat in an equal weight of butter and a
good splash of the best brandy.

Chop up the bones of the birds and put them in the roasting pan with ½
tablespoon of fresh butter and a generous seasoning of pepper. Cook on
the hob until well browned, then add the wine. Cook until reduced by two
thirds, then add the stock and continue to cook until the liquid has reduced
again by two thirds. Pass the sauce through a fine sieve, then whisk in the
intestine and butter purée to finish.

Quickly cook the mushrooms in a little butter and fry the slices of brioche
in butter. Serve the woodcock breasts and legs with the sauce, fried brioche,
mushrooms and truffle slices, then add the woodcock heads cut in half to
reveal the delicate, delicious brains.

SERVES 4

4 woodcock
1 tbsp vegetable oil
about 150g butter
good brandy
375ml good red wine,
    preferably Burgundy
260ml veal stock
    (see page 322)
100g white button
    mushrooms
8 slices of brioche
12 slices of cooked truffle
salt
black pepper

Faisan Archiduc

PHEASANT STUFFED WITH TRUFFLE AND FOIE GRAS

This is real cuisine bourgeoise – rich, opulent and satisfying. The cooking method ensures a moist and flavoursome bird and this recipe also works well with guinea fowl.

First prepare a rice pilaf for the stuffing. Preheat the oven to 200°C/Fan 180°C/Gas 6. Place an ovenproof pan on the hob, melt ½ tablespoon of the butter and sweat the onion until softened. Add the rice and stir to coat all the grains in butter, then pour in the chicken stock. Bring to the boil, then transfer the pan to the oven and bake for 20 minutes. Remove and set aside for 20 minutes.

When the rice is cool, gently mix in the foie gras, then add the pistachios, game jus and diced truffles. Season well.

Remove the wishbone from the pheasant and stuff the bird with the rice mixture, which should fill the cavity. Truss the bird to seal the neck and rear. Cover the bird with the slices of back fat and tie them securely in place. Preheat the oven to 200°C/Fan 180°C/Gas 6.

Heat the oil and remaining butter in a casserole dish and, when hot and foaming, add the bird and colour it on all sides. Place the dish in the oven with the bird breast-side up. After 10 minutes, add a spoonful of Madeira and put the lid on the casserole. Repeat this until the bird has been cooking for 40 minutes, then take the dish out of the oven, remove the fat and set the bird aside to rest.

Add the cream to the casserole dish and any juices that have run from the bird, then season. Put the dish on the hob, bring the liquid to the boil and reduce to a sauce consistency, then pass through a fine sieve. Spoon out the stuffing and carve the bird. Serve with the sauce, stuffing and some seasonal vegetables, such as braised cabbage.

SERVES 2

1½ tbsp unsalted butter
½ onion, peeled and
  chopped
40g long-grain rice
80ml chicken stock
  (see page 320)
100g cooked foie gras, diced
  (optional)
60g shelled pistachios
2 tbsp game jus
  (see page 329)
60g cooked truffles, diced
1 hen pheasant
thin slices of pork back fat
1 tbsp vegetable oil
4 tbsp Malmsey Madeira
  wine
200ml double cream
salt
black pepper

Suprême de pintade 'Paline'

BREAST OF GUINEA FOWL WITH ARTICHOKES AND BROAD BEANS

This is another adaptation of a great Escoffier classic. The tea gives a lovely smokiness to the cream that marries well with the flavour of the bird.

Blanch the broad beans in salted, boiling water, then refresh them in iced water and remove the husks. Put the beans in a food processor, heat the 80ml of double cream, then add it to the beans and blitz to a purée. Season with salt and pepper.

Prepare the artichoke hearts (see page 342), rubbing them with lemon to keep them white, then cook in salted, boiling water with a squeeze of lemon until tender. Drain and fill the artichokes with the broad bean purée. Top with a little of the cream (a tablespoon in all) and a sprinkling of Parmesan and brown the filled artichokes under a preheated grill for a few minutes.

Trim the guinea fowl supremes to neaten them up. Cut the ventrèche into 6 thick matchsticks. Using a skewer or small knife, push 3 matchsticks into each supreme, working diagonally through the meat.

Heat the butter and hazelnut oil in a pan until foaming. Add the supremes and cook them gently for 8–10 minutes, taking care that the butter doesn't burn and that the meat colours only slightly. Remove, cover and leave to rest.

Bring the tea and the remaining 2 tablespoons of cream to the boil, then reduce to make a very thick sauce. Cut the cooked ham into julienne strips and roll them in the sauce. Serve the guinea fowl with a few drops of the cooking butter, the ham with its sauce, and the artichokes.

SERVES 2

200g broad beans (shelled weight)
80ml double cream
6 small globe artichokes
1 lemon
3 tbsp double cream
1 tbsp grated Parmesan cheese
2 guinea fowl supremes
1 slice of ventrèche (or dry cured bacon), about 4cm thick
2 tbsp unsalted butter
1 tbsp hazelnut oil
2 tbsp very strong lapsang souchong tea (no milk)
2 slices of best-quality cooked ham (about 80g)
salt
black pepper

La volaille est pour la cuisine ce qu'est la toile pour les peintres

Poultry is for the cook what canvas is for the painter

JEAN ANTHELME BRILLAT-SAVARIN

Cailles aux raisins

QUAILS WITH GRAPES

I love the delicate flavour of quail and, prepared like
this with grapes and vine leaves, these little birds are
just exquisite. I prefer to serve quail on the bone and
attack them with my fingers, but if you want to make
the dish a little more elegant, remove the fillets and
present the meat off the bone.

Preheat the oven to 200°C/Fan 180°C/Gas 6. Cut the ventrèche into 4 and
put a piece inside each quail. Place a roasting tin on the hob and heat 2
tablespoons of the butter with ½ tablespoon of oil until foaming. Season the
quails and turn them in the butter and oil until golden, then place them in
the hot oven to roast for about 8 minutes until cooked but still pink. Remove
the quails from the tin and leave them to rest in a warm place.

Add a finely chopped shallot to the roasting tin and cook gently until
softened. Add the verjus and sugar, then the stock and simmer for a few
minutes. Pass the sauce through a fine sieve and stir in a tablespoon of
butter to finish the sauce. Check the seasoning.

Set aside 12 of the mushrooms and finely chop the rest. Heat ½ tablespoon
of oil in a pan with the remaining shallot, finely chopped, and the thyme
leaves, then add the chopped mushrooms. Once cooked, add a spoonful of
the sauce to moisten the mixture. Divide this between 4 of the vine leaves
and wrap them up into little parcels. Briefly sauté the whole mushrooms in
the remaining butter until tender.

Peel the grapes and remove any seeds if necessary. Just before you're ready
to serve, pat the remaining vine leaves dry. Pour some vegetable oil into a
frying pan to a depth of about 1cm and heat. Shallow fry the vine leaves until
crisp. Meanwhile, place the stuffed vine leaves in a steamer over simmering
water for a few minutes to reheat.

Serve the quail with the stuffed vine leaves and garnish with the button
mushrooms, fried leaves and a few grapes. If you have time, try fixing a few
green and red grapes on to one stalk.

SERVES 4 AS A STARTER
OR 2 AS MAIN COURSE

60g smoked ventrèche
   (or pancetta)
4 large quails
3½ tbsp unsalted butter
vegetable oil
2 shallots, peeled
50ml verjus (or light white
   wine if you can't find
   verjus)
1 tsp brown sugar
100ml brown chicken stock
   (see page 321) or veal stock
   (see page 322)
200g button mushrooms,
   wiped
1 sprig of thyme, leaves
   picked
8 vine leaves
small bunches of green and
   red grapes
salt
black pepper

Perdrix à la rôtissoire

PARTRIDGES ON THE ROTISSERIE

In France, this dish is cooked with thrushes in early autumn, when the birds have been gorging themselves on the remaining grapes on the vines, but in England you could use partridges. I always serve these with a few ceps and some thick slices of grilled baguette that have been rubbed with garlic and doused in olive oil.

Put the sultanas in a pan of cold water and bring to the boil, then drain and leave to cool.

Cut the brioche into 2cm cubes and douse them with a little milk and brandy until soaked. Peel the saucisson and cut it into 2cm cubes.

Stuff the cavity of each partridge with a few sultanas, cubes of brioche and saucisson. Thread the birds on to the rotisserie skewer, season and brush with a little olive oil. Cook gently until the skin is golden and the meat is cooked but still pink – this should take about 40 minutes, depending on how fierce the heat is or how near to the flame the birds are. Serve with ceps and grilled baguette as above.

Alternatively, preheat the oven to 220°C/Fan 200°C/Gas 7. Rub the stuffed partridges with butter and oil and roast for about 20 minutes. The meat should be cooked but still pink.

SERVES 4

1 tbsp sultanas or golden raisins
2 thick slices of brioche
enough milk to soften the brioche
brandy
200g good-quality saucisson
4 partridges, cleaned
olive oil
salt
black pepper

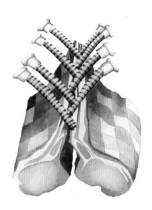

First and foremost, start with good-quality meat. Get
to know your butchers and talk to them about what
you're buying – use their knowledge and expertise.
Be adventurous and try some different meats now and
then, such as kid, wild boar and venison as well as the
more familiar beef and lamb. All are delicious and
well worth cooking. And don't be afraid of offal. Some
of the greatest of all French classics involve organ
meats such as brains and sweetbreads.

Viandes

Tête de veau revisitée

CALF'S HEAD, NEW STYLE

The modern method of preparing this classic French dish is lighter and more suited to modern tastes than the traditional version. Confit potatoes (see page 229) make a welcome accompaniment.

Mix the brine ingredients together. Make sure all the hair has been removed from the calf's head, then rub it, and the extra tongue, with brine. Cover and place in the fridge for 2 days.

Rinse the head and tongue well and rub them with lemon juice. Place them in a large pan with the onions, carrots, celery, bouquet garni and most of the rest of the lemon juice, cover with cold water and bring to the boil. Skim any scum off the surface, season, then reduce to a very low simmer and continue to cook until tender. Two hours should be about right.

Remove the head from the pan and drain, then lay it on a piece of cling film, skin-side down. Peel the tongues and put one of them along the centre of the head. Roll up the head in the cling film as tightly as possible and place it in the fridge overnight to set.

Put the sweetbreads in a pan of salted water with a squeeze of lemon, bring to the boil and cook for 15 minutes, then leave to cool. Drain the sweetbreads well and trim, then cut them into nuggets about the size of large walnuts. Dust with flour, then dip in the egg and finally roll in the breadcrumbs seasoned with salt and piment d'Espelette. Cut the remaining tongue into rectangles of about 1cm x 4cm and cut the calf's head into 1cm slices. Heat a little oil in a pan and sear the slices until warm and slightly crisp. Do the same with the tongue and the breaded sweetbreads.

For the shallot purée, cut the shallots in half, season well and place them in a roasting pan with the duck fat. Put them in a preheated oven, at 220°C/Fan 200°C/Gas 7, and cook until golden and soft. Blend them in a food processor with the duck fat until smooth.

To make the sauce, boil the veal jus, season and add the shallot, capers and piquillo peppers. Keep warm.

To serve, spread a generous spoonful of shallot purée on each plate and add the slices of calf's head, tongue and sweetbread. Add some sauce and sprinkle with herbs and chopped egg.

SERVES 8–10

1 calf's head, off the bone, with tongue
1 calf's tongue
juice of 2 lemons
2 onions, roughly chopped
2 carrots, roughly chopped
4 celery sticks, chopped
1 bouquet garni
2 veal sweetbreads
plain flour, for dusting
1 free-range egg, beaten
120g white breadcrumbs
2 tsp flaked piment d'Espelette (dried chilli flakes)
vegetable oil, for frying
salt
black pepper

BRINE

500g coarse sea salt
250g caster sugar
100g nitrate salt
1 sprig each of thyme and rosemary
1 bay leaf
1 tbsp juniper berries

SHALLOT PURÉE

8 shallots, peeled
1 tbsp duck fat

SAUCE AND GARNISH

180ml veal jus (see page 329)
1 shallot, finely chopped
2 tbsp fine capers
20g piquillo peppers, diced
1 hard-boiled egg, chopped
1 tbsp chopped chervil and tarragon leaves

Tête de veau ravigote

CALF'S HEAD, OLD STYLE

This is the traditional way to cook and serve calf's head and is still a best seller in the big bustling brasseries you find throughout France. The head is cooked in a solution called a *blanc* which is prepared with a tablespoon of flour per litre of water, plus salt and some vinegar or lemon juice. The blanc should then be covered with a layer of fat, such as beef or veal suet, to seal the pot and prevent oxidation and therefore discoloration of the item being cooked. This is an aficionado's way of eating calf's head – very filling and not for the faint-hearted! It's sometimes made with the brain poached separately and added to the dish on serving. It should be served with boiled vegetables and potatoes all in one big deep bowl, with sauce ravigote.

Make sure all the hair has been removed from the head, then put it in a huge pot and cover with cold water. Quickly bring the water to the boil, then drain and rinse clean. Rub the head with a cut lemon half.

Make the blanc by pouring cold water through a sieve into the pot and adding a tablespoon of flour per litre. Add salt (5 grams per litre), 2 tablespoons of lemon juice, the onion and the bouquet garni. Bring this to the boil, then leave to cool slightly. Add the calf's head, then bring to a gentle simmer and cover with a layer of beef or veal suet. You can use a wet tea towel instead of the suet if need be.

Cook the head for about 2 hours or until tender, then leave to cool. Drain, peel the tongue and cut the tongue and head meat into big chunks about 2–3cm thick – use everything, even the ears!

Make the sauce by mixing all the ingredients together. Cook the vegetables separately in salted water, then cut the carrots and leeks into large pieces.

Serve the meat piping hot with the vegetables and the ravigote sauce. If necessary, reheat the meat and the vegetables in a little of the blanc.

SERVES 12

1 calf's head with tongue, off the bone

1 lemon

1 tbsp of plain flour per litre of water

5g salt per litre of water

1 onion, peeled and studded with 2 cloves

1 bouquet garni, made up of leek, parsley stalks, bay leaf, thyme and celery (see page 342)

veal or beef suet

SAUCE RAVIGOTE

100ml vegetable oil

40ml white wine vinegar

1 tbsp fine capers

½ tbsp chopped curly parsley

2 tbsp mixed snipped herbs – chives, tarragon, chervil

1 white onion, peeled and finely chopped

salt

black pepper

VEGETABLES

4 carrots, peeled

2 leeks, trimmed

36 small new potatoes, scrubbed

Blanquette de veau

WHITE VEAL STEW

A wonderfully soothing dish, blanquette de veau is cooked in homes and restaurants in many parts of France. Traditionally, the meat for a blanquette was from a very fatty part of the belly and kept on the bone. For today's taste, it is more often cooked with a leaner cut and without the bone. Pilau rice is a good accompaniment.

Put the meat in a pan, cover generously with cold water and bring to the boil. Turn the heat down to a gentle simmer and skim any froth off the surface. After 30 minutes, add the vegetables, bouquet garni and a little salt. Continue to simmer for a further 80 minutes – you may need to top it up with boiling water.

While the meat is simmering, carefully decant about half a litre of the cooking liquid and pour it over the cocktail onions in a separate pan. Simmer until tender, then add the mushrooms. Cover and simmer for another 10 minutes until cooked. Now drain and pour the liquid back into the meat pan. Keep the onions and mushrooms warm in a tureen.

When the veal is tender, carefully remove it and put it into the tureen. Cover and keep warm. Discard the vegetables that were cooked with the meat.

Bring the cooking liquid to a rapid boil for 15 minutes or until reduced by half. Add the double cream, boil again for 5 minutes, then take the pan off the heat and stir in the whisked egg yolk and crème fraiche mixture. Check for seasoning and pour the sauce though a fine sieve over the meat and garnish. Serve at once.

SERVES 6—8

1kg boned breast of veal, cut into 4cm chunks
1 large onion, studded with 2 cloves
2 carrots, peeled
1 leek, white part only
1 bouquet garni, made up of leek, parsley stalks, bay leaf, thyme and celery (see page 342)
salt

GARNISH
24 small cocktail onions, peeled
250g small button mushrooms, wiped

SAUCE
300ml double cream
2 free-range egg yolks whisked with 2 tbsp crème fraiche
salt
white pepper

Côte de veau Pojarski

VEAL CHOPS, POJARSKI STYLE

In this dish, the meat is removed from the chops, minced and then reformed around the bones. Some would ask why bother mincing up a delicious piece of meat in this way? Just try it is my answer and you'll discover how delicious it is. Serve with a good meat jus, heightened with a little lemon juice. A classic dish, it may have been invented by a cook called Pojarski for Tsar Nicholas 1.

SERVES 4

2 double veal chops
100g unsalted butter
100g white breadcrumbs,
    soaked in 2 tbsp of cream
    until soft
plain flour
breadcrumbs
2 free-range eggs
vegetable oil (enough to
    shallow fry)
salt
black pepper

Take the meat off the chops and set the bones aside. Trim the meat and remove any sinew, then mince the meat with the butter and mix in the softened breadcrumbs. Season the mixture well, then shape it along each chop bone to reform the shape. Place the chops in the fridge to set.

Spread the flour and breadcrumbs on separate plates and whisk the eggs in a bowl.

Dust the chops with flour first, then dip them into the egg and lastly coat with breadcrumbs. Place the chops in the fridge again to chill and set before frying – don't be tempted to skip this step, as it is important that the chops are firm before frying.

Heat enough vegetable oil in a frying pan for shallow frying. Add the chops and gently brown them all over. Turn them carefully so that all of the breadcrumb coating is beautifully golden – you'll need to hold each chop with tongs to brown the edges.

Meanwhile, preheat the oven to 200°C/Fan 180°C/Gas 6. Place the browned chops in the oven for about 15 minutes or until the meat is cooked but still pink. Slice each chop in half and serve with some sautéed spinach.

Cervelle de veau zingara

CALVES' BRAINS ZINGARA

Calves' brains are considered a great delicacy in France and can be prepared in a number ways – I like to blanch the brains, then fry them until golden brown as in this recipe. Zingara means gypsy woman and to serve a dish *à la zingara* means with a sauce containing mushrooms, ham and tomatoes.

Rinse the brains in cold water, then put them in a saucepan and cover with cold water. Add a pinch of salt and a splash of vinegar to keep the brains white. Quickly bring the water to the boil, then immediately turn the heat down to a very gentle simmer for 5 minutes. Leave to cool, then gently remove the brains, drain them well and pat dry with a clean cloth.

Make sure the mushrooms are clean. Melt a tablespoon of butter in a pan, add the mushrooms and a squeeze of lemon, then cover and cook until tender. Cut the mushrooms into slices or matchsticks and keep the cooking liquid to add to the sauce. Cut the ham into pieces similar in size to the mushrooms. Dice the tomatoes.

To make the sauce, sweat the chopped shallots in a little butter, then deglaze the pan with the white wine. Add the mushroom cooking liquid and the veal jus, then reduce to a sauce consistency. Finish with a tablespoon of butter and seasoning, then add the mushrooms, ham, tomato and finally the snipped tarragon. Keep warm.

Using a small knife, remove any sinew from the brains and cut them into slices. Dust in seasoned flour and gently fry the brains in a tablespoon each of oil and butter until golden brown – 3 or 4 minutes on each side. Serve with lots of the sauce and the potatoes.

POMMES MACAIRE

Preheat the oven to 200°C/Fan 180°C/Gas 6. Wash the potatoes, place them on a bed of rock salt in a baking tray and bake for 40 minutes or until cooked. Leave to cool, then cut them in half and scoop out the flesh. Mash the flesh with a fork and add the 30g of butter, cream, herbs, egg yolk and seasoning. Shape into little potato cakes about 5cm across by 2cm high, dust with flour, then fry in oil and butter until golden and hot.

SERVES 4

2 calves' brains
white wine vinegar
20 firm white button
    mushrooms, wiped
unsalted butter
1 lemon
4 slices of ham
4 plum tomatoes, peeled and
    deseeded
2 shallots, peeled and
    chopped
2 tbsp white wine
250ml veal jus (see page 329)
leaves from a bunch
    tarragon, snipped
plain flour, seasoned with
    salt and pepper
vegetable oil
salt
black pepper

POMMES MACAIRE (POTATO
    CAKES)

2 baking potatoes
rock salt
30g unsalted butter, plus
    extra for frying
2 tbsp double cream
1 tbsp snipped chives
1 tbsp chopped flatleaf
    parsley
1 free-range egg yolk
plain flour, for dusting
oil, for frying
salt
black pepper

Ris de veau braisé au safran

BRAISED SWEETBREAD WITH SAFFRON

This is one of my mother's recipes and something she used to cook for my sister and me as a special treat. Even now I ask my mum to make this dish and the smells and flavours take me right back to my childhood. I prefer the pancreas or 'heart' sweetbread, as it is bigger and rounder and makes nicer nuggets. Great served with home-made pasta but it's fine to use bought if you prefer.

If making your own pasta, mix all the ingredients by hand or in a mixer to make the dough. Leave to rest until needed.

Put the sweetbread in a pan of cold water, add salt and the juice of half a lemon, then simmer for about 7 minutes. Leave to cool.

Drain the sweetbread and trim off all the sinew, then break it up into nuggets. Dust in a little flour and then pan fry in half a tablespoon of butter and the oil, until golden.

Remove the sweetbread nuggets and set them aside, then drain the excess fat from the pan. Add a knob of fresh butter, then the shallots and carrots. Sweat for a few moments, then deglaze the pan with the wine, and boil to reduce. Add the chicken stock, saffron and cream, then put the sweetbread nuggets back in the pan and simmer gently until fully cooked, basting and turning frequently. Check the seasoning, adding a squeeze of lemon if necessary.

Meanwhile, roll out the pasta dough and cut it into ribbons. Cook in plenty of boiling water, then drain and toss in a little butter.

Serve the sweetbread in deep bowls with the pasta and plenty of the rich creamy sauce.

SERVES 2

1 veal sweetbread (pancreas or 'heart')
1 lemon
plain flour, for dusting
unsalted butter
1 tbsp vegetable oil
2 shallots, peeled and chopped
2 carrots, peeled and sliced or diced
1 glass of sweet white wine
100ml chicken stock (see page 320)
generous pinch of saffron strands
100ml double cream
salt
black pepper

PASTA

250g plain flour
2 free-range eggs
3 free-range egg yolks
½ tbsp olive oil
salt

Langue de boeuf au persil et câpres

SALTED OX TONGUE WITH CAPER PARSLEY SAUCE

Tongue is a great favourite of mine and this piquant sauce sets it off to perfection. If you like salt beef you will enjoy this too, although the texture is different and even more delicious. Great served hot like this or cold in a sandwich with some pickles. Keep any leftover stock for making soup.

Rinse the tongue in cold water, place it in a large pan and cover with cold water. Bring to the boil, then drain and rinse the tongue again.

Put the tongue back in the pan and add the carrot, onion, celery and herbs. Bring it to a very gentle simmer, cover with greaseproof paper and cook until tender – about 2 hours. Leave the tongue to cool in the liquor and then remove it, peel off the skin and carve it into slices. Keep the cooking liquor for the sauce.

To make the sauce, melt the butter in a small pan, stir in the flour, then add 200ml of the cooking liquor and the cream. Cook for 10 minutes. Press the sauce through a fine sieve, then add the parsley and capers along with a squeeze of lemon juice if you like. Serve hot with the sliced tongue and boiled potatoes.

SERVES 8

1 salted ox tongue
1 carrot, peeled
1 onion, peeled and studded
   with 2 cloves
1 celery stick
2 bay leaves
1 sprig of thyme

CAPER PARSLEY SAUCE

50g unsalted butter
1 tbsp plain flour
200ml cooking liquor
125ml double cream
2 tbsp chopped flatleaf
   parsley
2 tbsp capers
lemon juice

Côte de boeuf rôtie

ROAST RIB OF BEEF

I like my beef hung for 21 days on the bone. Most
butchers hang meat for 7–14 days, but the extra week
ensures tenderness and gives the meat a greater depth
of flavour. Fore rib has a vein of fat running through it
that melts as it cooks to keep the meat beautifully moist.
When you buy your beef, ask your butcher what breed it
is from, as this is important. The various breeds, such
as pure Aberdeen Angus, Dexter and Charolais, all have
their own particular taste and texture so try them all
and discover your favourite.

SERVES 2

1 rib of beef (500–600g
    with the bone)
olive oil
flaked sea salt
black pepper

Preheat the oven to 220°C/Fan 200°C/Gas 7. Season the beef, then heat a
roasting pan over a high heat and seal the beef all over in a little olive oil.
Place it in the oven and roast for 8 minutes – the meat should be rare.
Leave to rest out of the oven for 10 minutes before carving. Sprinkle the
slices of beef with a little flaked sea salt before serving.

Serve the beef with some Béarnaise sauce (see page 331), roast potatoes
and green vegetables.

Pot-au-feu

POACHED BEEF STEW

One of the ultimate French classics, this could well be my father's all-time favourite dish... or at least one of them! He likes to eat it with some sauce Albert (see page 148) on the side. When properly made, pot-au-feu is the most succulent winter feast and good enough to grace any table. A purée of sweet parsnips is a good accompaniment, but the vegetables cooked in the stock and the sauce are more than enough. The leftovers can be the foundation of a wonderful soup or a warm salad, dressed in a mustard shallot vinaigrette.

Section the oxtail into pieces through the joints and trim any gristle off the tongue. Place both with the beef shin in a large pan of cold water and bring to the boil, then drain and rinse. Put everything back into the pan and add the boiling chicken or chicken wings – if using wings, tie them in a muslin cloth. Cover generously with cold water and add the 2 tablespoons of salt.

Set the pan over a high heat and as soon as it comes to the boil, turn the heat down until there is barely a tremor on the surface – it should be about 90°C. Add the peppercorns, bouquet garni, garlic and washed celery. Cut an onion in half and blacken the cut side on a dry griddle pan, then add it to the pot with the other onion studded with 2 cloves. Continue to simmer very gently for 90 minutes, skimming when needed. At the end of the 90 minutes, remove the chicken or the wings, then put the pot back on the heat. The chicken is really just to flavour the stock, although you can strip the meat off the carcass and use it in a pie or mayonnaise salad.

Wrap the carrots and turnips in a muslin cloth. Tie the cabbage and leeks together securely with string. Add these to the pot and cook for 30 minutes. Decant just enough of the liquid to cover the peeled potatoes in a separate pan and simmer until cooked. Poach the bone marrow in a little stock.

After about 2½ hours in total the meat should be tender. Leave to cool a little before carefully removing it from the pan. Slice the shin. Peel the outer skin of the tongue, then slice. You can leave the oxtail on the bone or pick the meat off. Serve in deep bowls with the hot vegetables and steaming hot clear cooking stock, with some sauce Albert on the side. Serve the poached marrow on slices of toasted baguette sprinkled with sea salt.

SERVES 6

1 oxtail

1 veal tongue

500g shin of beef (boned weight), tied

1 free-range boiling chicken or 12 chicken wings

2 tbsp fine salt

12 white peppercorns

1 bouquet garni, made up of leek, parsley stalks, bay leaf, thyme and celery (see page 342)

4 garlic cloves

½ head of celery, cut from the root

2 onions, peeled

2 cloves

6 Chantenay carrots, peeled

6 turnips, peeled

1 small savoy cabbage, cut in half

4 small leeks, washed and trimmed

6 small potatoes, peeled

200g veal bone marrow

6 slices of baguette bread

coarse sea salt

Boeuf Bourguignon

BRAISED BEEF IN BURGUNDIAN WINE

Some recipes suggest marinating the beef for 24 hours or more, but I find this makes for a gamey flavour that's not entirely true to the original. Like all braised dishes, this is best eaten a day or two after it's made – simmer gently to reheat and add the garnish just before serving so that it's bright and fresh. Boiled potatoes are the classic accompaniment but mash is more to my taste.

Pour the wine into a saucepan and boil until reduced by half. Trim the beef and cut it into 3cm cubes, then dust with flour. Heat a frying pan until very hot, add a dash of oil and brown the beef well on all sides. Do this in batches so you don't overcrowd the pan. Preheat the oven to 160°C/Fan 140°C/Gas 3.

Once all the beef has been browned and set aside, discard the oil and add a tablespoon of clean oil, the sliced onion and crushed garlic. Cook until the onion is brown and caramelised, then put the meat back in the pan. Add the brandy, followed by the reduced wine, and simmer for 2–3 minutes.

Pour everything into a cast-iron casserole dish, then season and add the bouquet garni and stock. Bring to a simmer, skim well to remove any surface scum and cover loosely with a lid or greaseproof paper. Place in the oven and cook until the meat is tender – this should take 1½–2 hours, depending on the cut. Leave to cool, then take the meat out of the dish and set aside. Skim to remove any fat, then pass the liquid through a sieve into a pan. Boil until it thickens to a sauce, then add the meat. Cover and chill until needed.

To prepare the garnish, melt a tablespoon of butter in a saucepan and add the onions, seasoning, 2 tablespoons of the sauce from the beef and 4 tablespoons of water. Braise the onions until they are shiny and cooked through. Put the carrots in a pan with just enough water to cover and most of the rest of the butter. Season and bring to a gentle boil, then cook until almost all the liquid has evaporated and the carrots are tender and shiny with butter. Brown the strips of bacon in a frying pan. Sweat the mushrooms in a little butter until cooked but still firm and add seasoning and lemon juice.

To serve, gently reheat the boeuf bourguignon on the hob while you prepare the garnish. Add a couple of knobs of cold butter to enrich and shine the sauce, then garnish with the onions, carrots, bacon and mushrooms. Take the dish to the table for everyone to admire, then serve in wide bowls.

SERVES 4

1 bottle of red Burgundy wine
700g braising beef (chuck is good but cheek is best)
plain flour, for dusting
vegetable oil
1 onion, peeled and sliced
2 garlic cloves, peeled and crushed
60ml brandy
1 bouquet garni, made up of thyme, bay leaf and parsley stalks (see page 342)
400ml beef or veal stock (see pages 322–323)
2 tbsp cold unsalted butter
salt
black pepper

GARNISH

3 tbsp unsalted butter
12 brown-skinned cocktail or button onions (or small shallots), peeled
12 young carrots, peeled
120g smoked streaky bacon rashers or ventrèche, cut into thin strips
12 button mushrooms, wiped
juice of ½ lemon

L'ail est à la sante ce que le parfum est à la rose

Garlic is to health what the rose is to fragrance

PROVENÇAL PROVERB

Filet de cheval grillé comme au bistro

GRILLED HORSE FILLET, BISTRO STYLE

In most of mainland Europe horsemeat is considered a delicacy and was certainly always a treat in my family. It is slowly gaining popularity in England and I now serve it in the restaurant. This is a simple recipe that shows off the rich, slightly gamey flavour of the meat, which must be of excellent quality. Lovely served with game chips (see page 229) as well as the shallots.

SERVES 2

2 large banana shallots
1 x 400g horse fillet
olive oil
coarse salt
black pepper

Preheat the oven to 200°C/Fan 180°C/Gas 6. Put the shallots on a baking tray and roast them for 30 minutes.

Smear the horse fillet with a little oil, then lightly season with salt and pepper. Grill on a griddle or grill pan over a high heat, turning to mark it evenly all over. Transfer it to an oven tray and put it in a preheated oven at 220°C/Fan 200°C/Gas 7 for 8 minutes for medium rare, depending on the thickness of the meat. Leave to rest for 5 minutes before carving and sprinkling with a little coarse salt. Cut the shallots in half and serve them with the meat and some game chips if you like.

Chevreau grillé Provençale

GRILLED KID, PROVENCE STYLE

Like new season's lamb, kid (young goat) is a traditional
Easter treat in the south of France and the milky white
meat lends itself to Provençal flavours. My preferred
way to cook kid is to poach it first, then grill it on a
charcoal grill or barbecue. Otherwise, cook the kid in
the oven and finish it under the grill to get a lovely crisp
golden brown exterior.

Place the leg and shoulder in a pan, cover with cold water and season with
salt. Add the onion, 2 of the bay leaves, the sarriette, 6 cloves of garlic, the
dried chilli split in half and the parsley stalks, saving the leaves for later.
Bring to the boil, then turn the heat down and simmer the meat very gently
for 10 minutes. Take the pan off the heat and leave to cool.

Chop the remaining garlic and bay leaves and put them in a bowl with the
chopped parsley leaves, chilli powder, honey, green and black olives, olive
oil, anchovies, lemon zest and juice, and spring onions. This should make a
thick sauce, but add a little of the cooking liquid if you need to moisten it.

Blitz a third of the sauce to form a paste in a blender – I like to leave the rest
chunky to serve with the meat. Remove the kid from the stock and pat it dry.
Lightly score the skin with a thin-bladed, sharp knife and rub some of the
paste on to the meat. Cover and repeat after an hour.

If using a charcoal grill or barbecue, it's important to cook the meat slowly
and gently. Dip the rosemary fronds into the remaining paste and use them
to baste the meat regularly, until it is golden and crisp on the outside and
succulent within. Over a gentle heat it should take no more than 45 minutes.
If cooking in the oven, cook at 200°C/Fan 180°C/Gas 6 – the time will be
about the same.

Serve with some roasted baby new potatoes and a few salad leaves. The sauce
will be sufficient dressing.

SERVES 4–6

1 leg of kid on the bone
1 shoulder of kid
1 onion, peeled and
    quartered
4 bay leaves
1 bunch of sarriette (summer
    savory)
1 garlic bulb
1 piment d'Espelette (whole
    dried chilli)
1 bunch of parsley
1 tsp ground piment
    d'Espelette (chilli powder)
2 tbsp acacia honey
60g green olives, pitted and
    chopped
60g black olives, pitted and
    chopped
200ml olive oil
6 salted anchovy fillets,
    chopped
zest and juice of 1 lemon
2 spring onions, thinly sliced
2 sprigs of rosemary
salt
black pepper

*Un bon repas doit
commencer par la faim*

A good meal ought to begin with hunger
FRENCH PROVERB

Gigot d'agneau de sept heures

LEG OF LAMB COOKED FOR SEVEN HOURS

This is a very special dish, prepared over a time span of more than a week, but there is surprisingly little work involved and the flavour is amazing. The recipe does appear in my Gavroche cook book but it is a great favourite and one I wanted to include here.

Trim the lamb, remove the aitch bone and lightly score the skin – your butcher will do all this for you. Cut 12cm-long strips of pork back fat and use these to lard the lamb lengthways at least 6 times with a knife or a larding needle.

Mix all the marinade ingredients together, add the lamb and cover with cling film. Place in the fridge and leave to marinate for a week, turning the meat several times a day so it all absorbs the flavours.

Drain the lamb, reserving the liquid and the vegetables. Heat the butter and oil in a thick-based braising pan, add the lamb and cook over a medium-high heat until golden brown. Remove the lamb from the pan and if the fat is burned, discard it and use fresh butter to cook all the vegetables (including the marinade vegetables) until golden brown. Add the bacon, then deglaze the pan with the wine, port and marinade. Place the pan over a high heat and reduce the liquid by two thirds, then add the lamb, season well and cover with the veal stock. Bring to the boil and skim. Check the seasoning. Put a lid on the pan and place it in the oven at 140°C/Fan 120°/Gas 1 for approximately 7 hours! Keep an eye on it, though, as ovens vary and you may have to top up the liquid with some water occasionally. Also, the cooking time may vary depending on the age and quality of the lamb. The meat should be tender and nearly falling off the bone.

Take the lamb out of the oven and leave it to cool in the sauce. When the lamb is cold, remove it from the pan and strain the sauce through a fine sieve. Check for seasoning and consistency – reduce the sauce if necessary. Pour the sauce over the meat and leave it in the fridge overnight.

The next day when you're ready to serve, reheat the meat gently in the sauce in a pan on the hob, while basting occasionally. Bring it to the table and serve with a spoon – don't attempt to carve. Good with mashed potatoes.

SERVES 8

1 x 3kg leg of lamb
200g pork back fat
100g unsalted butter
2 tbsp olive oil
1 onion, peeled and sliced
1 carrot, peeled and sliced
1 celery stick, chopped
150g smoked bacon
2 bottles of full-bodied red wine
½ bottle of port
3 litres veal stock (see page 322)
salt
black pepper

MARINADE

½ bottle of full-bodied red wine
2 garlic cloves, crushed
1 small onion, peeled and thickly sliced
1 carrot, peeled and thickly sliced
1 sprig of thyme
1 sprig of rosemary
2 tbsp extra virgin olive oil
2 cloves
1 tbsp white peppercorns
3 tbsp brandy
2 tbsp red wine vinegar

Carré d'agneau rôti Provençale

ROAST RACK OF LAMB

Always leave a little fat on a new season's lamb rack
to enhance the beautiful sweet flavour. Serve with a
traditional ratatouille (see page 214)and roast potatoes
with garlic (see page 226). Ask your butcher to French
trim the rack so the bones are beautifully clean.

Preheat the oven to 220°C/Fan 200°C/Gas 7 and season the lamb. Heat
the oil in an ovenproof pan on the hob and sear the lamb over a high heat,
fat-side down, until golden. Turn the lamb over and continue to cook for
another 2–3 minutes.

Add the garlic and thyme, then place the pan in the preheated oven for
16 minutes for pink lamb, basting twice. Take it out and leave the meat
to rest in a warm place.

Drain the fat from the pan, add the shallot and cook gently over a moderate
heat. When it is soft, add the stock and boil until syrupy. Remove the garlic
and thyme, then whisk in the cold butter to finish the sauce. Carve the lamb
and serve with ratatouille and roast potatoes.

SERVES 2

1 rack of lamb, French
  trimmed
2 tbsp vegetable oil
2 garlic cloves, bruised
1 sprig of thyme
1 shallot, peeled and finely
  chopped
150ml veal stock (see
  page 322)
50g cold unsalted butter
salt
black pepper

Gigot d'agneau en croûte de sel

LAMB IN A SALT CRUST

Baking meat in a herby salt crust keeps it beautifully
moist and brings a lovely scented flavour to the meat.
The crust itself is not eaten.

To make the salt dough, put all the ingredients in a large bowl and bring
them together by hand, then knead the dough for no more than a couple
of minutes. Leave it to rest in the fridge for at least 2 hours before using.

Season the lamb and put it in a roasting pan over a high heat with a little
olive oil. When it is golden and sealed all over, remove it from the heat
and leave it to cool slightly.

Put the bread in a food processor with the herbs and whizz to make fine
green breadcrumbs. Roll the lamb in the crumbs, pressing them on firmly.

Preheat the oven to 200°C/Fan 180°C/Gas 6. Dust your work surface very
lightly with flour, then roll out the salt dough to a thickness of about 1cm.
If the dough cracks or breaks, you should be able to reshape it as it is fairly
pliable. Place the lamb on the dough and fold it over to wrap and seal the
meat completely. Beat the whole egg and egg yolk together and brush over
the dough to glaze and seal the seam. Bake in the oven for 35 minutes.

Remove the lamb from the oven and leave it to rest for at least 20 minutes.
Put the lamb jus into a small pan and boil to reduce by about one-third.
Whisk in the butter a little at a time.

To serve, cut open the crust, remove the meat and carve. Serve with the
enriched jus and some vegetables such as baby turnips.

SERVES 3–4

1 leg of milk-fed lamb,
   boned (about 800g
   boned weight)
olive oil
6 slices of day-old rustic
   white bread, crusts
   removed
3 sprigs of flatleaf parsley
3 sprigs of tarragon
flour, for dusting
1 free-range egg
1 free-range egg yolk
200ml lamb jus
   (see page 329)
50g cold unsalted butter,
   diced
salt
black pepper

SALT DOUGH
250g fine table salt
400g coarse sea salt
1kg plain flour
2 free-range egg whites
400ml lukewarm water
roughly chopped thyme,
   rosemary, lavender
   and sage

Filet de porc aux morilles

PORK FILLET WITH CREAMED MORELS

This creamy morel sauce can be used for any white meat but I find it goes particularly well with pork.

Preheat the oven to 200°C/Fan 180°C/Gas 6. Put the pork in a roasting pan with a little oil and roast for 10 minutes, turning occasionally so it colours evenly. The meat should be cooked, but still pink and moist. Remove it from the pan and set aside to rest in a warm place while you make the sauce. Be sure to collect any juices from the meat and add them to the sauce at the end.

Discard the fat from the roasting pan and place the pan over a medium heat. Add the butter and shallots and sweat for about 2 minutes, until tender. Add the morels and sweat for a further 2 minutes. Pour in the Madeira and scrape the bottom of the pan with a wooden spoon to loosen any caramelised bits. Bring to the boil and reduce by two-thirds, then pour in the cream and reduce to a light sauce consistency. Season with salt and pepper.

Slice the pork fillet and serve with the morel sauce and perhaps some plain or wild rice or mashed potatoes to mop up the sauce.

SERVES 4

1 fillet of organic pork (about 900g trimmed weight)
olive oil
40g unsalted butter
4 shallots, peeled and finely chopped
400g fresh morels, trimmed and washed
1 tbsp Madeira wine
300ml double cream
salt
black pepper

Choucroute

PORK WITH SAUERKRAUT

This is a traditional Alsace feast. There are quite a few variations but they are always based around different cuts of pork. I have seen choucroute served with tail, snout — which I particularly love — and every morsel in between. The more mainstream versions include frankfurters, a more meaty sausage such as a Morteau, as well as knuckle or gammon and belly, all heaped over a steaming pile of pickled cabbage and cooked either in beer or white Alsatian wine. Boiled potatoes are a must. I have also come across choucroute de la mer — cabbage with an assortment of seafood — and I must say I'm quite partial to this too!

Rinse the knuckles or gammon in cold water and place them in a deep pan with the belly. Cover with cold water and bring to a gentle simmer, then skim well and add the onions, spices and bay leaves. Cook for 75 minutes, then add the Morteau sausages and continue to cook for another 15 minutes. Turn off the heat and cover the pan with a cloth or greaseproof paper.

Ladle out enough of the liquid to cook the potatoes in a separate pan until tender. Reheat the cabbage in a saucepan by gently simmering it with the Riesling wine and a little of the pork cooking liquid. Five minutes before serving reheat the frankfurters in the pan with all the other pork and serve piping hot.

Serve the meat and potatoes in big bowls on top of the hot cabbage.

SERVES 8—12

3 green pork knuckles, salted or 1kg green gammon
1kg pork belly in 1 piece
2 onions, peeled and halved
10 juniper berries
12 black peppercorns
2 bay leaves
2 Morteau, or similar, sausages
16 medium potatoes, peeled
1kg choucroute (pickled cabbage), precooked
300ml Riesling wine
8 frankfurters

Selle de lapin farcie aux pruneaux

SADDLE OF RABBIT STUFFED WITH PRUNES

This is a classic dish from the Aquitaine region, where some of the best prunes are grown and they make wonderful brandy too. I like to serve it with a gratin Savoyard as well as the braised lettuce. Unless you are confident of your butchery skills, ask your butcher to bone out and trim the saddle of rabbit, keeping it intact. You also need the liver and kidneys for cooking with the lettuce.

Open out the saddle of rabbit and set the liver and kidneys aside for later. Season the meat with salt and pepper and place the prunes in a row down the middle. Roll up the saddle neatly and wrap it tightly in cling film to make a sausage. Tie it securely with string. Bring a pan of seasoned water to simmering point, add the rabbit and poach for 8 minutes.

Leave the rabbit to cool a little, then remove the cling film. Heat most of the butter in a frying pan until foaming, then roast the rabbit in the pan for 4–5 minutes, until golden. Remove it and set aside to keep warm. Add the chopped shallots to the pan, then pour in a splash of brandy to deglaze. Stir well, scraping up all the sticky bits, then add the veal stock and cook until reduced and thickened. Stir in the rest of the butter to finish the sauce.

For the braised lettuce, cut the little gem into quarters and season. Fry it briefly in a knob of butter until lightly coloured and just cooked but still crunchy. Add the rabbit liver and kidneys and sear them quickly in a little butter until browned but still pink inside.

To serve, cut the rabbit into thick slices and place on warm plates with the lettuce, liver and kidneys and sauce. Turn out a gratin on to each plate.

GRATIN SAVOYARD

Cut the potatoes into neat rounds. Heat the butter and oil in a pan with the garlic and herbs, then fry the potatoes until cooked and golden. Remove and pat them dry. Boil the cream in a small pan until reduced by half. Preheat the oven to 200°C/Fan 180°C/Gas 6. Take a couple of small chef's rings, about 4cm high. Starting with potato, build the gratins with alternating layers of potato, cream and cheese, finishing with cream and cheese. Bake for 5–6 minutes, then glaze them under a hot grill.

SERVES 2

1 saddle of rabbit, boned, with liver and kidneys
6 soft prunes, stones removed
100g unsalted butter
3 shallots, peeled and chopped
splash of brandy
250ml veal stock (see page 322)
salt
black pepper

BRAISED LETTUCE
1 little gem lettuce
unsalted butter

GRATIN SAVOYARD
2 potatoes, peeled (Roosters are ideal)
1 tbsp unsalted butter
1 tbsp oil
1 garlic clove, peeled and crushed
1 sprig of thyme
2 bay leaves
100ml double cream
40g Gruyère cheese, grated

Selle de lapin rôtie aux poireaux et sauce à la bière

ROAST SADDLE OF RABBIT WITH ALE SAUCE AND LEEKS

This is a traditional robust country dish, full of great flavours. I like to cook and serve the rabbit on the bone – it might not look very elegant but the meat stays tender and juicy. The kidneys should be attached to the saddles so just leave them on to cook with the rabbit.

Bring a pan of salted water to the boil. Blanch the leeks until tender, then remove them and refresh them in iced water. Drain and slice them into rounds about 1cm thick.

Preheat the oven to 220°C/Fan 200°C/Gas 7. Heat a tablespoon of oil in a cast-iron casserole dish and brown the seasoned rabbit until golden on all sides. Add a tablespoon of butter and the onion, then place the casserole dish in the oven for 15 minutes. Remove the rabbit saddles from the dish and leave them to rest in a warm place.

Put the casserole dish back on the stove and pour in the ale, lemon juice and treacle. Boil until almost dry, then add the stock and simmer for 10 minutes.

Whisk a tablespoon of butter into the sauce, then pass it through a fine sieve and season to taste. Pan fry the leeks in a non-stick pan with a little oil and butter until brown, or brown them on a ridged grill pan. Serve the rabbit with the leeks, sauce and roast potatoes.

SERVES 4

2 large leeks, trimmed and washed (or baby leeks in season)
vegetable oil
4 saddles of rabbit, on the bone with kidneys
unsalted butter
1 medium onion, peeled and sliced
100ml good brown ale
1 tbsp lemon juice
1 tbsp treacle
200ml chicken stock (see page 320)
salt
black pepper

Carpaccio de chevreuil

VENISON CARPACCIO

Carpaccio is Italian in origin, but we have a tradition of serving raw meat in France and we've taken this dish to our hearts. It's an excellent way to serve good venison and extremely easy to prepare. The most difficult part is slicing the meat really thinly. You'll need a good sharp knife or a slicing machine – a piece of kit that's readily available now, not too expensive and useful for a number of tasks. If you don't have time to freeze the meat, put it in the freezer until firm and almost frozen, then remove and slice.

Check that your venison has been nicely trimmed and there are no traces of fat or sinew. Freeze the venison, then take it out of the freezer about half an hour before you want to serve.

Shave the vegetables into fine strips using a Japanese mandolin, then place them in iced water to curl and crisp. To make the horseradish cream, whip the cream until firm and fold in the horseradish and a pinch of salt. Whisk the ingredients for the dressing together.

Cut the meat as thinly as possible and arrange overlapping slices on each plate.

Drain the vegetables well and add some to each plate along with the cheese and a spoonful of horseradish cream. Drizzle with the dressing and sprinkle over the mixed shoots.

SERVES 4 AS A STARTER

360g fillet of venison, trimmed weight
2 small turnips, peeled
4 breakfast radishes
4 thin slices of Berkswell sheep's cheese
mixed herb shoots

HORSERADISH CREAM
100ml whipping cream
60g fresh horseradish, grated
salt

DRESSING
1 tbsp balsamic vinegar
2 tbsp olive oil
salt
black pepper

Gigue de chevreuil rôtie à la Chevigné

ROAST LEG OF VENISON WITH PEARS, CHESTNUTS AND PEPPER SAUCE

Venison is available almost all year round and it's a great alternative to beef for a family roast. I think it's best in the winter months and this rich pepper sauce is a classic accompaniment. You need to start this dish well before you want to eat it, as the meat has to marinate for two days.

To make the marinade, crush the juniper berries, peppercorns and bay leaves in a pestle and mortar and add the olive oil, wine and brandy. Using a larding needle, thread the strips of pork fat evenly through the venison. If you don't have a needle, make cuts with a long thin knife and push the fat into them with your finger. Put the meat in a plastic bag with the marinade, seal and refrigerate for 2 days, turning and massaging it occasionally.

To make the sauce, warm the oil in a frying pan and cook the shallots until caramelised. Add the peppercorns and redcurrant jelly and stir until the jelly has melted, then pour in the vinegar and let it boil away. Pour in the wine and port and cook until the liquid is reduced by half. Add the stock and reduce by half again, then pass the sauce through a fine sieve into a clean pan. Season, place over a medium heat and whisk in 2 tablespoons of butter.

For the garnish, heat 2 tablespoons of the butter until foaming, then add the pears and cook them gently until golden and tender. Drain off a little of the butter, then add the honey to give the pears a gloss and shine. Finish with a squeeze of lemon juice and season with salt and pepper.

Preheat the oven to 200°C/Fan 180°C/Gas 6 and bake the shallots for 20 minutes, then leave to cool. Remove the skins and cut the shallots in half, then fry them in a non-stick pan with a tablespoon of butter until golden and caramelised. Season. Bring the cream to the boil, add the chestnuts, then blitz in a blender until smooth. Add the remaining 2 tablepoons of butter to add gloss to the purée. Season as necessary.

Take the meat out of the fridge at least an hour before cooking. Preheat the oven to 230°C/Fan 210°C/Gas 8. Drain the venison, place it in a roasting tin and rub the oil into the meat. Season it well and put it in oven. After 20 minutes, turn the heat down to 200°C/Fan 180°C/Gas 6 and continue to cook for 40 minutes for pink meat. Remove the venison and let it rest for at least 20 minutes before carving and serving with the hot sauce, garnished with the cooked pears, shallots and chestnut purée.

SERVES 6

4 juniper berries
6 black peppercorns
2 bay leaves
2 tbsp olive oil
100ml red wine
2 tbsp brandy
200g pork back fat,
    cut into long strips
    about 5mm thick
1 x 4kg leg of venison on the
    bone
2 tbsp vegetable oil

SAUCE POIVRADE (PEPPER
    SAUCE)
1 tbsp vegetable oil
6 shallots, peeled and sliced
1 tbsp crushed white and
    black peppercorns
1 tbsp redcurrant jelly
3 tbsp red wine vinegar
300ml full-bodied red wine
100ml port
600ml game stock
2 tbsp unsalted butter

GARNISH
5 tbsp unsalted butter
4 Comice pears, peeled and
    quartered
2 tbsp honey
1 lemon
4 banana shallots
125ml double cream
200g cooked chestnuts
    (vacuum packed are fine)
salt
black pepper

Cuisine n'est pas chimie. C'est un art. Elle exige instinct et le goût plutôt que des mesures exactes

Cookery is not chemistry. It is an art. It requires instinct and taste rather than exact measurements

MARCEL BOULESTIN

Epaule de sanglier braisée, crème de cassis pimentée

BRAISED SHOULDER OF WILD BOAR WITH PEPPERED CASSIS SAUCE

There are now wild boar all over France, even in the suburbs of some major cities. The meat is delicious when slow cooked, and I particularly enjoy the shoulder on the bone. I have a regular supply of wild boar from my brother-in-law Gérard, who shoots them in the Cévennes hills. Farmed boar is now available in many butchers and tastes good, but might not need to be cooked for quite so long. Start this the day before you want to eat it as the meat needs to marinate for 24 hours. Barley risotto is an excellent accompaniment.

SERVES 6

1 x 4–5kg wild boar shoulder
3 tbsp red wine vinegar
3 tbsp brandy
3 tbsp olive oil
2 bay leaves
2 piments d'Espelette
   (whole dried chillies),
   cut in half
8 garlic cloves, peeled
2 onions, peeled and sliced
200ml crème de cassis
300ml water
salt
black pepper

Make small incisions with a sharp knife all over the boar shoulder. Place it in a plastic bag and add the vinegar, brandy, oil, bay leaves and piments d'Espelette. Seal the bag and leave the meat to marinate in the fridge for 24 hours.

When you're ready to cook, preheat the oven to 220°C/Fan 200°C/Gas 7. Take the meat out of the bag and drain off the marinade – set it aside for later, including the chillies and bay. Season the meat, place it in a roasting tin and put it in the preheated oven for 30 minutes. Then add the peeled garlic, sliced onions, the marinade and crème de cassis, turn the oven down to 160°C/Fan 140°C/Gas 3 and cook for a further 10 minutes. Add 300ml water, cover loosely with foil and continue to cook for a further 4 hours until the meat is tender and falling off the bone.

The cooking liquid should be of sauce consistency, but if not, transfer it to a pan and boil until reduced and syrupy. You may need to skim off a little fat. I prefer to leave the garlic, onions and chilli in the sauce but if you want it silky smooth, press it through a fine sieve. Carve the meat and serve with the sauce and barley risotto (see page 251).

Tête de sanglier sauce mousquetaire

CRISPY WILD BOAR HEAD WITH SPICY SHALLOT MAYONNAISE

This can also be made with ordinary pork but it's particularly good with wild boar. The head needs to be shaved and singed to remove all the bristles, then taken off the bone. If this is beyond your talents the butcher should be able to oblige.

Take the head, lay it out flat, with the skin-side down, on your work surface and season. Mix the garlic, mustard, rosemary and thyme and spread this evenly over the meat. Then roll the head up neatly and tie tightly with string. Place it in a pan, cover well with cold water and bring it to the boil. Skim well, add the celery, carrot, onion, bay, peppercorns and some salt, then turn down the heat so the water is barely simmering. Cook gently for 2–3 hours, depending on the size of the head, until the meat is tender and until easily pierced with a skewer.

Leave the meat to cool in the cooking liquid, then take it out and roll it tightly in cling film. Refrigerate overnight. Pass the stock through a sieve and use it for a soup another time.

For the sauce, simmer the finely chopped shallots in the wine until all the liquid has evaporated. Add the stock and continue to cook until the shallots are soft and the liquid sticky. Season with salt, pepper and a generous amount of cayenne, then leave it to cook a little.

Make a mayonnaise with the yolks, mustard and vinegar and slowly whisk in the oil. Once made, add the shallot mix and check the seasoning. The sauce should have a good kick and be a little sharp.

When you're ready to eat, cut the head into 2cm slices and then remove the string and cling film – they help to keep everything in place as you slice. Heat a tablespoon of vegetable oil and fry the slices until crispy on both sides. Serve with the mayonnaise and some roast vegetables.

SERVES 10–12

1 wild boar head, 2–3kg boned weight
1 garlic clove, peeled and very finely chopped
1 tbsp Dijon grain mustard
1 tbsp mixed chopped rosemary and thyme leaves
1 celery stick
1 carrot, peeled
1 onion, peeled
2 bay leaves
1 tbsp black peppercorns
1 tbsp vegetable oil
salt

SPICY SHALLOT MAYONNAISE

2 shallots, peeled and finely chopped
125ml dry white wine
125ml veal stock (see page 322)
good pinch of cayenne pepper
2 free-range egg yolks
1 tbsp Dijon mustard
1 tbsp white wine vinegar
250ml vegetable oil
salt
black pepper

Escargots à la Chartreuse et noisettes

SNAILS WITH CHARTREUSE AND HAZELNUTS

I remember being dragged out into the fields with my father and mother to collect snails after a heavy shower. We purged (fasted) the snails for several days and washed them in copious amounts of salted water. They then had to be boiled, removed from the shell, intestines trimmed off and finally bottled and preserved for later use. Thankfully you can now buy jars or cans of very good-quality precooked snails, with all the hard work already done – though I look back on those days with much fondness.

Drain the snails. Sweat the finely chopped shallots and garlic in the olive oil until tender, then add the hazelnuts, followed by the snails. Add the butter and continue to cook gently for 6–7 minutes.

Pour in the Chartreuse, turn up the heat and boil until the pan is almost dry. Add the cream and simmer until the mixture has the consistency of a sauce. Season well and finish with a few drops of lemon juice and a little finely grated zest. Serve in little pots with a sprinkling of parsley.

SERVES 6 AS A STARTER

6 dozen snails (canned are fine)
3 shallots, peeled and finely chopped
3 garlic cloves, peeled and finely chopped
2 tbsp olive oil
3 tbsp chopped hazelnuts
20g unsalted butter
2 tbsp green Chartreuse
500ml whipping cream
lemon juice
grated lemon zest
2 tbsp chopped parsley
salt
black pepper

Vegetables are treated with proper care and respect in the French kitchen. Not only do they partner fish or meat but they can also be the stars of many dishes and the basis of a whole meal. Seasonality is all important. Go to the market in a French town and you will find vegetables that are growing in the region, rather than items imported from many different parts of the world. Salads are not just for garnish and can be stand-alone dishes – try the smoked duck and cabbage on page 248 for example. Lighter salads are usually served after the main course.

Légumes
et salades

Ratatouille

MEDITERRANEAN VEGETABLE STEW

For this Provençal dish to taste its best all the
vegetables must be cooked separately before being
combined for the final stage. All too often ratatouille
is an indeterminate mush, but when properly prepared
with ingredients at the peak of their summery
perfection, it can be a joy. Delicious warm or cold.

Dice the aubergine, courgettes, pepper, onion and tomatoes – large or
small, as you prefer – keeping them in separate piles. Heat about 1cm of
olive oil in a pan over a high heat and colour each type of vegetable, except
the tomatoes, individually, then drain them in a colander.

Preheat the oven to 200°C/180°C/Gas 6. Place all the vegetables in an
ovenproof dish or large pan and add the diced tomatoes, garlic, thyme, bay
leaves and tomato paste. Season and cover with greaseproof paper. Place in
the preheated oven for about 20 minutes or so until all the vegetables are
tender. If you prefer, you can do this on the hob over a gentle heat. Lovely
served with rack of lamb (see page 192).

SERVES 4

1 aubergine

2 courgettes

1 red pepper, peeled and
  deseeded

1 large onion, peeled

2 tomatoes, peeled and
  deseeded

olive oil

1 bulb of new season garlic,
  chopped

1 sprig of thyme

2 bay leaves

2 tbsp tomato paste

salt

black pepper

Gâteau Savoyard aux pommes de terre et lard

POTATO, PRUNE AND BACON CAKE

A traditional country-style recipe from the Savoie region of France, this can be served as an accompaniment for a roast or as a stand-alone dish with dandelion salad. Some recipes use prunes, others sultanas, but I like to include both. The shape is important not only for presentation but also for the cooking. Traditionally, this is baked in a Kugelhopf mould or the fluted mould for the sweet gâteau de Savoie, but you can use an ordinary 20cm cake tin.

SERVES 6

1.4kg baking potatoes
2 onions, peeled and finely
  sliced
16 plump soft prunes, stoned
80g sultanas
26 thin rashers of streaky
  bacon
unsalted butter, for greasing
salt
black pepper

Peel the potatoes and grate them coarsely, then place them in a cloth and squeeze them dry. Tip the grated potatoes into a bowl, then add the finely sliced onions, prunes, sultanas and a generous amount of seasoning and mix together well.

Preheat the oven to 180°C/Fan 160°C/Gas 4. Line the mould with the bacon rashers, making sure they overlap a little and hang over the sides of the mould. Pack in the potato mixture and fold the overhanging bacon over the top. Place the mould in a bain-marie or a roasting tin and pour in enough boiling water to come halfway up the sides. Cover with some buttered foil and bake for 2 hours.

Allow the gâteau to cool a little before turning it out of the mould – it will fall apart if you try to turn it out right away. Wonderful hot or cold.

Gratin de macaronis au potiron

BAKED MACARONI WITH SQUASH

Use butternut or any other kind of winter squash to make this dish, which goes beautifully with roast game and other meats or can be served on its own. Meat stock is best as it helps to glue the pasta together, but you could use vegetable stock to make a vegetarian version.

SERVES 4

800g mixed squash, cut into wedges
olive oil
6 amaretti biscuits, crushed
250g dried macaroni
60g unsalted butter
300ml veal stock (see page 322)
200ml double cream
50g Parmesan cheese, grated
30g salted almonds, chopped
salt
black pepper

Preheat the oven to 200°C/Fan 180°C/Gas 6. Put the squash in a baking tray, drizzle it with olive oil and bake in the oven for about 30 minutes or until tender. Scrape all the flesh off the skin and mash it with a fork, then season well and add the crushed amaretti.

For cooking the macaroni you need a pan large enough to hold all the pieces in a single layer. Heat the butter in the pan until it is foaming, then add the macaroni. Roll them in the butter until they are golden on all sides, then add the stock and bring to a simmer. Season and continue to cook until the pasta is tender and the stock has almost completely evaporated; add a little water if necessary.

Place the macaroni side by side on a piece of greaseproof paper – it's important that they are tightly packed together – and smear any liquid that's left over the top. Put them in the fridge for about an hour to set. Once set, cut the macaroni into 8 small circles of about 8cm across or to fit the dishes or chef's rings you are going to use. Boil the cream until it thickens, then season with salt and pepper.

Preheat the oven to 200°C/Fan 180°C/Gas 6. Place 4 dishes or chef's rings on a baking sheet and place a circle of macaroni in each one, followed by some squash and a generous amount of cream. Repeat the layers, finishing with a circle of macaroni, then top with cream, grated Parmesan and chopped almonds. Bake in the oven for about 10 minutes to reheat, then colour the top under a hot grill. Carefully remove from the dishes or rings and serve the gratins as an accompaniment to a main course or as a starter with a few bitter leaves.

Salade Lyonnaise

DANDELION AND BACON SALAD

The classic salade Lyonnaise is made with dandelion leaves and if you are lucky enough to have a garden with an untreated area in it, you can pick your own. However, dandelions can taste a little bitter to some people so you can use frisée salad, or curly endive, if you prefer.

Pick through the salad leaves, then wash and dry them carefully. Cut the bacon into strips or batons, place them in a non-stick pan with a drop of olive oil and cook slowly over a medium heat.

Cut the baguette into about 20 slices, 1cm thick. Drizzle them with olive oil, then bake in a preheated oven at 200°C/Fan 180°C/Gas 6 for about 15 minutes or until crisp. Rub with a cut clove of garlic.

Put a saucepan of water on to boil with a generous splash of white wine vinegar. Crack the eggs and carefully drop them into the simmering, vinegared water to poach. The eggs should take about 4 minutes for the whites to be cooked, but the yolks should still be runny.

Put the salad leaves in a bowl and pour the golden-brown bacon and fat on top. Add the bread, red wine vinegar and remaining olive oil, season lightly with salt but generously with pepper, then toss. Serve the salad on to plates and place the drained, hot eggs on top. Serve immediately.

SERVES 6

400g dandelion leaves or
   frisée salad
180g smoked streaky bacon
4 tbsp olive oil
1 small baguette
2 garlic cloves
white wine vinegar
6 free-range eggs
2 tbsp red wine vinegar
salt
black pepper

Artichauts vinaigrette

ARTICHOKES VINAIGRETTE

Globe artichokes were a real treat for me as a child, but I remember my English friends coming round for dinner and being quite scared when they saw these alien things on the plate. I loved the sheer delight and fun of tearing off the leaves, dipping them into the vinaigrette, and finally drawing the leaf through clenched teeth to leave a morsel of deliciously deep-flavoured artichoke. When all the leaves have been chewed, only the heart and the inedible choke is left. This needs to be lifted or scraped out with a spoon. Add another drizzle of vinaigrette and one of the most classic and satisfying starters is complete.

Snap off the stems and place the artichokes in a deep pan. Cover with cold water and add a pinch of salt and the lemon quarters. Bring the water to the boil and simmer the artichokes gently for 30–40 minutes. You may need to put a plate on top of the artichokes to keep them submerged. Take the artichokes out of the water and drain, then check they are done by pulling off a couple of leaves.

Whisk all the vinaigrette ingredients together and serve with the artichokes. I think they are best served warm, but you can put them in the fridge and eat them the next day.

SERVES 4

4 large globe artichokes
pinch of salt
1 lemon, cut into quarters

VINAIGRETTE

25ml olive oil
75ml vegetable oil
2 tsp Dijon mustard
25ml white wine vinegar
salt
black pepper

*Je veux l'ordre et le goût. Un repas
bien affiché est renforcé à cent
pour cent à mes yeux*

I want order and taste. A well-displayed meal
is enhanced one hundred per cent in my eyes

ANTONIN CARÊME

Pommes de terre rôties à l'ail

ROAST POTATOES WITH GARLIC

I like to use a cast-iron pan for cooking these potatoes (right), which go perfectly with a rack of lamb.

Wash and drain the potatoes well. Heat the oil in a cast-iron pan until smoking, then add the potatoes. Cook until light golden brown all over, then add the garlic, thyme and butter. Turn down the heat and loosely cover the potatoes with greaseproof paper, then cook gently for 10 minutes until tender. Season, drain off the fat and tip the potatoes into a bowl to serve.

SERVES 4

180g small new potatoes, peeled
2 tbsp vegetable oil
6 new season garlic cloves, in their skin
a few sprigs of thyme
1 tbsp unsalted butter
salt
black pepper

Pommes boulangère

POTATOES COOKED WITH STOCK AND ONIONS

This dish is named after the baker because the tradition was to cook it in the bakery oven once all the bread was done. The residual heat ensured a lovely long and slow cooking time for this delicious potato dish. Excellent served with roast pork or white meats.

Peel the potatoes and cut them into slices of about 2–3mm thick. Do not wash them. Peel and thinly slice the onions. Heat the oil and a tablespoon of the butter in a frying pan, add the onions and fry until soft but not coloured. Add them to the potatoes, season well and spread everything in an ovenproof dish. Preheat the oven to 200°C/Fan 180°C/Gas 6.

Pour the stock into the dish, add the thyme and place in the oven for 35 minutes. Melt the remaining butter. Take the dish out, press down on the potatoes with a slotted spoon, then brush the top with the melted butter. Put the potatoes back in the oven for 10 minutes to crisp up.

SERVES 8

1kg red potatoes, such as Roosters
2–3 onions
1 tbsp vegetable oil
2 tbsp unsalted butter
250ml chicken stock (see page 320)
1 sprig of thyme
salt
black pepper

Pommes gaufrettes

GAME CHIPS

These crispy waffle-style chips (left) can be cut on a
mandolin with a waffle blade. Perfect with good plain
meat such as grilled fillet of horse (see page 187).

Peel the potatoes, then slice them as thinly as possible on a mandolin. Rinse
in cold water, then drain and pat dry.

Heat the duck fat or dripping in a deep-fat fryer and fry the game chips a
batch at a time until golden and crispy. Drain and season with a little salt.

SERVES 2–3

2–3 chipping potatoes, such
   as Roosters
1kg duck fat or dripping, for
   frying
salt

Pommes de terre confites

GRILLED POTATOES COOKED IN DUCK FAT

Confit potatoes, slowly cooked in delicious duck fat,
go beautifully with tête de veau revisitée (see page 168),
among other dishes.

Peel the potatoes and, using a sharp knife, trim them into cylinder shapes
with a flat top and bottom. Cook them briefly on a hot ridged grill until they
are nicely marked with the grill lines.

Melt the duck fat in a pan and add the potatoes – they should be submerged
in the fat. Cook for about 25 minutes or until tender. Season with a little salt.

SERVES 6–8

8 potatoes, such as Maris
   Pipers or Roosters
200g duck fat
salt

Ragoût de morilles

MOREL AND CELERIAC STEW

For me, morel mushrooms are the best of all mushrooms. When they're out of season I use the dried variety which have an intense woody, musky scent that works beautifully with cream sauces, Madeira and white meats. With fresh morels, a lighter preparation is better, so I like to stew them gently in good butter with some diced celeriac and tomato.

Trim and wash the mushrooms, then leave them on a cloth to drain thoroughly.

Peel and dice the celeriac and blanch it in boiling, salted water for a few seconds. Refresh in iced water, then drain and place with the morels.

Heat a tablespoon of butter in a pan and sweat the shallots until tender. Add the morels and celeriac, then turn up the heat a little and cook for 4–5 minutes until the mushrooms have softened. Add the lemon juice, the rest of the butter and seasoning. Just before serving, add the diced tomato and a few basil leaves.

SERVES 4

200g fresh morels
100g celeriac
2 tbsp unsalted butter
2 shallots, peeled and
    chopped
juice of 1 lemon
1 large plum tomato,
    blanched, skinned
    and diced
basil leaves
salt
black pepper

Salade d'asperges

ASPARAGUS SALAD

Seeing the first asparagus in the market is a joy and means that spring is most definitely with us. The white variety favoured by those in northeastern Europe, including Alsace, is delicious but in my view not as flavoursome and versatile as the luscious green or purple variety. Here are three of my favourite sauces to go with asparagus. Always serve warm or at room temperature but never cold, as this blunts the taste.

Take the asparagus and bend the stalk of each one until it snaps, then discard these woody ends. Peel the stalks using a peeler and wash the asparagus if necessary.

Tie the asparagus in bundles and cook in boiling, salted water until tender, then refresh in iced water to stop the cooking and retain the colour. Drain well and serve with your chosen dressing or sauce.

VINAIGRETTE AUX HERBES ET OEUF DUR

Mix the oil, vinegar, mustard and seasoning, then fold in the herbs and chopped eggs.

SAUCE MALTAISE

Blanch the orange peel in plenty of boiling water for one minute, then drain. Chop finely, then put it in a small pan with the juice and sugar and boil until syrupy. Leave to cool a little, then add to the hollandaise

CRÈME FOUETTÉE À LA TRUFFE

Whisk the cream into soft peaks. Add the crème fraiche, lemon juice and seasoning, then the grated truffle.

SERVES 4

1.2kg asparagus
  (untrimmed weight)
salt

VINAIGRETTE AUX HERBES
  ET OEUF DUR

60ml extra virgin olive oil
15ml red wine vinegar
1 tbsp Dijon mustard
2 tbsp mixed snipped fresh
  herbs (tarragon, parsley,
  chives, chervil)
2 free-range eggs, hard-
  boiled and chopped
salt
black pepper

SAUCE MALTAISE

thinly pared peel of 1 orange
juice of 3 oranges
20g brown sugar
1 quantity of hollandaise
  sauce (see page 330)

CRÈME FOUETTÉE À LA
  TRUFFE (TRUFFLE
  DRESSING)

150ml whipping cream
1 tbsp crème fraiche
juice of 1 lemon
60g truffle, grated (canned
  are fine)

Bombine Ardèchoise

POTATOES AND CEPS, ARDÈCHE STYLE

This is a traditional dish in the Ardèche region of France and there are as many versions as villages! Every family has their own recipe, but this is my favourite. Delicious on its own or a perfect accompaniment to a roast chicken.

If using fresh ceps, wipe them clean, then slice. If using dried ceps, soak them in cold water until soft and reconstituted.

Boil the potatoes in salted water until tender, then drain, peel and slice. Blanch the mangetout in boiling water, then plunge them into iced water to stop the cooking and keep their colour. Cook the French beans in the same way.

Heat the duck fat or oil in a heavy-based frying pan until smoking hot. Add the sliced potatoes and fry, turning them frequently until beautifully golden brown all over. Turn down the heat, add the ceps, shallots, mangetout and French beans, then season with salt and black pepper. Cook for 2 minutes, add the garlic and parsley, then mix and serve immediately.

SERVES 4

200g fresh ceps or
    60g dried ceps
16 new potatoes
150g mangetout, trimmed
100g French beans, trimmed
3 tbsp duck fat or olive oil
2 shallots, peeled and
    chopped
2 garlic cloves, peeled and
    finely chopped
1 tbsp chopped parsley
salt
black pepper

Salade bagatelle

CARROT AND ASPARAGUS SALAD

This colourful salad combines the lovely sweetness of the young carrots, with a sharp peppery kick from the watercress. It is a classic, usually served as an accompaniment to a main course.

Mix the ingredients for the dressing together and set aside.

Take the asparagus and bend the stalk of each one until it snaps, then discard these woody ends. Peel the stems with a peeler and wash if necessary. Peel the carrots.

Tie the asparagus in bundles and cook them in boiling, salted water until tender, then refresh in iced water to stop the cooking and retain the colour. Drain well and cut on an angle into 5mm slices. Cook the carrots until tender, then refresh and slice.

Toss the carrot and asparagus with dressing to taste, then finish with a little watercress also dipped in the dressing. Just before serving, sprinkle the sliced mushrooms on top.

SERVES 4

2 bunches of large green asparagus
4 new season carrots
2 bunches of watercress, washed and dried
12 white mushrooms, wiped and sliced

DRESSING
½ tbsp Dijon mustard
1 tbsp white wine vinegar
4 tbsp olive oil
salt
black pepper

La salade Aveyronnaise

WARM SALAD WITH SWEETBREADS AND ROQUEFORT

L'Aveyron in the Midi-Pyrénées is where one of the greatest of all blue cheeses is made – Roquefort. This pungent, salty, creamy ewe's milk cheese is shown off to good effect in this delicious warm salad.

Trim, wash and dry the salad leaves.

To blanch the sweetbreads, put them in a pan of salted water, bring to the boil and cook for 6 minutes. Drain and rinse under cold water. Peel the membrane off the sweetbreads, then roll them in the seasoned flour. Heat a tablespoon of oil with the butter in a frying pan, add the sweetbreads and fry until brown and crispy.

Warm the crème fraiche in a pan, then whisk in the Roquefort until it melts. Season with a little salt and pepper.

Add the thinly sliced shallot to the salad leaves and toss with the lemon juice, remaining oil, salt and pepper. Spoon some Roquefort cream on to each plate and add the warm sweetbreads and salad on top. Serve at once.

SERVES 4

250g mâche (corn salad)
100g escarole (curly endive)
180g lamb's sweetbreads
plain flour, seasoned with
    salt and pepper
3 tbsp vegetable oil
1 tbsp unsalted butter
3 tbsp crème fraiche
80g Roquefort cheese
1 shallot, peeled and thinly
    sliced
juice of ½ lemon
salt
black pepper

Salade caprice de reine

ENDIVE, APPLE AND TRUFFLE SALAD

When Le Gavroche and The Waterside Inn first opened, salads were always offered as side dishes with all main courses, never as a starter. On some of the earlier menus *salade du jour* also featured and most were as elaborate as this recipe.

Cut the endive into manageable bite-sized strips. Remove the leaves from the celery and set them aside for garnishing the salad, then cut the celery heart into strips about the same size as the endive. Put the endive and celery in iced water for 20 minutes to firm up, then drain well.

Peel the apples and cut them into matchsticks, then put them into a little water and lemon juice to keep them white.

Mix the mayonnaise with the crème fraiche in a serving bowl and season with salt and pepper and the remaining lemon juice.

Put the endive, celery and apple sticks in a bowl and garnish with thin shavings of truffle. Serve with the mayonnaise and crème fraiche sauce to spoon over.

SERVES 6

200g Belgian endive
1 head of celery, tender
    heart only
3 eating apples (such as
    Golden Delicious)
juice of 1 lemon
2 tbsp mayonnaise
    (see page 332)
2 tbsp crème fraiche
60g fresh or cooked truffles
salt
black pepper

Salade de betterave aux noix

BEETROOT AND WALNUT SALAD

There are many varieties of beetroot in different colours but the best ones for this recipe are the long, carrot-shaped 'crapaudine' variety, which has a superior flavour, and the beautiful stripy chioggia beets. If you cannot find these particular types, use large, normal red beetroot. I prefer to bake beetroot, especially for salads, as this intensifies their taste and natural sweetness.

Preheat the oven to 200°C/Fan 180°C/Gas 6. Bake the washed beetroot as you would bake a potato – this should take about 30–40 minutes.

Meanwhile, if you have time, skin the walnuts by soaking them in a little boiling milk, then peeling them with the point of a small knife. This is a fiddly job but worth the effort, as the skin can leave a bitter tannic taste. Mix the mustard, red wine vinegar and walnut oil to make the dressing and season with salt and pepper.

When the beetroot are cool enough to handle, peel them, cut them into a mixture of cubes and thin slices and douse them with some of the dressing while still lukewarm – beetroot soak up dressing better if not fridge cold.

Fold in the sliced shallots, parsley and a little more dressing if necessary just before serving, then garnish with the walnuts.

SERVES 4

4 large beetroot
16 walnut kernels
milk
½ tbsp Dijon mustard
1 tbsp red wine vinegar
4 tbsp walnut oil
2 shallots, peeled and finely sliced
1 tbsp coarsely chopped flatleaf parsley
salt
black pepper

Salade pomone

FRISÉE, APPLE AND GRUYÈRE SALAD

I'm not sure of the orgins of this salad but it is one of my favourites. The combination of bitter salad leaves, crunchy tart apple, sweet spicy mustard and cheese is divine. Savora mustard is an aromatic mustard that's popular in the north of France.

SERVES 4

1 head of frisée salad
4 russet apples
1 lemon
4 tbsp olive oil
1 tbsp white wine vinegar
½ tbsp Savora mustard
100g Gruyère cheese, grated
1 tbsp snipped chives
salt
black pepper

Pick through the frisée salad, then carefully wash and drain the leaves. Peel the apples and cut them into 5mm dice. Put these in a bowl of water with a squeeze of lemon to keep them white.

To make the dressing, mix the oil, vinegar, mustard, salt and pepper. Toss the salad leaves with the apple, grated cheese and dressing, then sprinkle the snipped chives on top.

*Les animaux se repaissent,
l'homme mange; l'homme d'esprit
seul sait manger*

Beasts feed, man eats; only wise
men know the art of eating
JEAN ANTHELME BRILLAT-SAVARIN

Gratin de cardons

BAKED CARDOON AND BONE MARROW

The cardoon belongs to the artichoke and thistle family and grows wild in the Mediterranean region where it has been eaten since Greek and Roman times. It's still a popular vegetable in parts of France – my wife's family always grow cardoon and serve it stewed with tomato sauce. This particular recipe is a Lyonnaise speciality and can be served as a starter, an accompaniment or even as a main dish. Choose a cardoon that feels heavy and discard the first layer of stalks, which tend to be stringy and hollow.

Peel the stalks of the cardoon as you would celery, removing the strings and any discoloured parts. Cut into manageable pieces about 16cm in length and put them in a saucepan. Add cold water, running it through a fine sieve containing the flour. This makes what is called a *blanc* in French culinary parlance and helps to keep the cardoon white. Add the lemon juice and a little salt.

Bring the water to the boil, then cover with a piece of greaseproof paper and simmer for about an hour until the cardoon is tender. Drain and cut the cardoon into bite-sized diamond shapes.

Preheat the oven to 220°C/Fan 200°C/Gas 7. Arrange a neat layer of cardoon on the base of individual heatproof dishes or one large dish. Sprinkle with a little Gruyère layer followed by some beef jus, then repeat the layers twice more. Finish with some slices of truffle and bone marrow, then top with the rest of the Gruyère. Place in the hot oven for 6–7 minutes, then finish under the grill for a lovely brown top.

SERVES 6

1 cardoon
1 tbsp plain flour
juice of 1 lemon
60g Gruyère cheese, grated
3 tbsp beef jus
  (see page 328)
20g cooked truffle,
  thinly sliced
100g veal bone marrow,
  cut into 5mm slices
1 tbsp unsalted butter,
  for greasing dishes
salt
black pepper

Salade jardinière

GARDEN SALAD

This is a deliciously light summery salad that's just right for lunch in the garden or to freshen the palate after a meaty main course.

Wash, peel and prepare the vegetables. Cut the turnip and carrot into 3mm-thick batons and trim the beans and cauliflower florets. Bend the stalk of each asparagus stalk until it snaps, then discard these woody ends. Peel the stalks using a peeler and wash if necessary.

To make the vinaigrette, whisk all the ingredients together. You'll have more than you need for this recipe, but the dressing keeps well in an airtight jar and can be used for other salads.

Cook the vegetables separately in boiling, salted water until al dente, then refresh them in iced water. Drain and dry well, then dress with the vinaigrette. Finish with a sprinkle of chervil and tarragon leaves.

SERVES 4

2 medium-sized white turnips
1 large carrot
60g French beans
100g cauliflower florets
1 bunch of asparagus
80g peas, shelled weight
chopped fresh chervil and tarragon

VINAIGRETTE
25ml olive oil
75ml vegetable oil
2 tsp Dijon mustard
25ml white wine vinegar
salt
black pepper

Tarte tatin de légumes

ROAST VEGETABLE TART

This is a wonderful stand-alone starter or main course and also makes a good accompaniment to a plain roast. Apple tarte tatin is a classic dessert but this sweet savoury take on the original is just as enjoyable. It can be made in a suitably sized ovenproof frying pan or in individual pans if you prefer. Vary the vegetables according to your taste and what's in season.

Preheat the oven to 220°C/Fan 200°C/Gas 7. Cut the vegetables into 3–4cm pieces and spread them on a baking sheet. Season and drizzle them with olive oil, then roast in the hot oven for 8–10 minutes. The vegetables should be partly cooked and have a little colour. Leave the oven on.

Melt the butter in an ovenproof pan, then sprinkle on the sugar. Put the cooked vegetables, sliced chilli (deseeded if you like) and thyme leaves on top, making sure to pack the vegetables tightly.

Roll out the pastry to about 3mm thick and place it over the vegetables, taking care to tuck it under them around the edges. Make a few holes in the pastry with the point of a knife, then bake the tart in the oven – still at 220°C/Fan 200°C/Gas 7 – for 20 minutes. Leave the tart to cool a little before turning out and serving.

SERVES 4

2 Belgian endives, trimmed
1 carrot, peeled
1 small parsnip, peeled
1 medium turnip, peeled
1 large onion, peeled
2 tbsp olive oil
2 tbsp unsalted butter
2 tbsp caster sugar
1 red chilli, sliced
leaves from 1 sprig of thyme
200g all-butter puff pastry
salt
black pepper

Salade tiède de choux au canard fumé

WARM CABBAGE SALAD WITH SMOKED DUCK

A pointed spring cabbage is good for this salad or even sliced large Brussels sprouts. Serve as an accompaniment to duck confit or as a starter, perhaps with a fried duck egg perched on top.

Remove the fat from the smoked duck, chop it up and place it in a pan with a tablespoon of the duck fat. Cook over a medium heat for 30 minutes until the pieces have rendered their fat and are crispy, like pork scratchings. Remove, leaving the melted fat in the pan, and keep warm.

Slice the cabbage and shallot very thinly and mash the garlic to a paste. Add the remaining duck fat to the pan and fry the cabbage, shallot and garlic over a medium to high heat. You want the cabbage to take on a little colour but keep it slightly underdone. Season, add the thinly sliced smoked duck breast and the pieces of crispy fat, then finish with the vinegar.

If serving with an egg, fry it in a little duck fat to make the dish even more ducky and indulgent.

SERVES 4

1 smoked duck breast
2 tbsp duck fat
1 pointed spring cabbage
   (about 360g)
1 shallot, peeled
1 garlic clove, peeled
1½ tbsp red wine vinegar
salt
black pepper

Riz à la Valencienne

RICE WITH HAM, MUSHROOMS AND ARTICHOKES

This versatile rice dish can be eaten as a starter or as an accompaniment to poultry or sausages. It can even be chilled, then drizzled with a little vinaigrette and served as a summer salad. Either way it's a delicious combination of tastes. You can use the preserved artichokes sold in good Italian delis.

Cook the mushrooms in ½ tablespoon of the butter and a little lemon juice until tender. Drain them, then slice and set aside. Add the cooking liquid to the chicken stock.

Preheat the oven to 200°C/Fan 180°C/Gas 6. Melt a tablespoon of butter in an ovenproof pan and sweat the chopped onion until soft and lightly coloured. Add the rice, stir well, then add the diced ham and the stock. Bring to the boil, then cover with a piece of greaseproof paper and place in the oven for 25 minutes. Remove and leave to rest for 5 minutes. The rice should have absorbed all the liquid.

Add the sliced artichokes, cooked mushrooms and remaining butter to the rice. Season with a little paprika, salt and pepper and fluff up with a fork before serving.

SERVES 4

12 small mushrooms, wiped
2 tbsp unsalted butter
juice of 1 lemon
460ml chicken stock
    (see page 320)
1 large onion, peeled and
    chopped
160g long-grain rice
40g cured ham, diced
4 small cooked artichokes,
    sliced
paprika
salt
black pepper

Orge perlé façon risotto

BARLEY RISOTTO

Lots of grains can be cooked like a risotto and make a change from rice. This version makes a perfect accompaniment to game dishes that are served with lots of sauce. The ground almonds add a touch of sweetness.

Drain the barley. Melt a tablespoon of the butter in a pan and sweat the finely chopped onion until translucent. Add the barley and continue to cook for 4–5 minutes, then add the picked thyme leaves and the wine. When the liquid has almost evaporated, add enough of the hot stock to cover and continue to simmer gently.

Cook as a rice risotto, adding more hot stock a little at a time and stirring frequently. The barley should absorb all the stock and you might need to add a little more liquid, depending on how dry it is.

After about 30 minutes of gentle cooking the barley should be tender so take the pan off the heat and fold in the ground almonds, Parmesan, remaining butter and seasoning.

SERVES 6

200g pearl barley, soaked in water for 2 hours
2 tbsp unsalted butter
1 onion, peeled and finely chopped
1 sprig of thyme, leaves picked
125ml dry white wine
600ml chicken stock (see page 320)
60g ground almonds
60g Parmesan cheese, grated
salt
black pepper

Sweet things are a treat and can be enjoyed at any time – not only at the end of a meal. They are an unnecessary indulgence but should bring pleasure and a smile. Pâtisserie does not have to be complex to be good, although some of the more elaborate recipes will be sure to impress, but a good pastry, lovingly prepared from great ingredients, will always be welcome at any table. France does have its regional specialities in desserts as in other dishes, but common to all regions is the use of local and seasonal produce.

Desserts

Tarte aux poires Bourdaloue

PEAR AND ALMOND TART

Probably my favourite fruit tart, this is simply
irresistible – especially when served warm. The name
may come from a street in Paris, rue Bourdaloue where
there was a famous pâtisserie, and the street in turn was
named after Louis Bourdaloue, a 17th-century French
Jesuit. Whatever the origins of its title, this confection
of poached pears, almond cream and crisp pastry is an
absolute delight.

Peel the pears, cut them in half and remove the cores. Pour about 300ml
of water into a large pan and add the vanilla pod, cinnamon stick and sugar.
Bring to the boil, then add the pears and simmer them for 20 minutes.
Leave to cool. You can do all this the day before making the tart if you like.

To make the pastry, cut the butter into small pieces and leave it to soften
at room temperature. Sift the flour and salt, place them on the work
surface and make a well in the centre. Add the butter and sugar and gently
work together with your fingertips. Add the egg yolk and gradually draw
in the flour, adding drops of water as you go. When all the flour has been
incorporated, shape the dough into a ball, but do not overwork it. Wrap
the pastry in cling film and refrigerate for at least 2 hours before using.

For the almond cream, whisk the butter and sugar until pale, then add the
ground almonds. Whisk in the eggs, one at a time, and finally the rum.

Preheat the oven to 200°C/Fan 180°C/Gas 6. Roll out the pastry on a floured
surface to a thickness of about 3mm and use it to line a greased 28cm flan
tin. Prick the pastry base with a fork, line it with greaseproof paper and fill
with baking beans, then bake blind for 20 minutes. Remove the paper and
beans and put the pastry back into the oven for another 5 minutes or until
the base has cooked but not taken on too much colour. Leave the oven on.

Spoon the almond cream into the tart base, then arrange the sliced,
drained pears on top, with the pointed ends towards the centre. Bake
in the preheated oven for 40 minutes.

When the tart is cooked, warm some apricot jam with a little water and
brush it over the surface. Sprinkle the tart with toasted sliced almonds
and serve warm.

SERVES 8

POACHED PEARS
4 pears (Williams are good)
about 300ml water
1 vanilla pod, split
1 cinnamon stick
250g caster sugar

SWEET PASTRY
80g unsalted butter
130g plain flour, plus extra
    for dusting
pinch of salt
30g sugar
1 free-range egg yolk
1 tbsp water

ALMOND CREAM
125g softened unsalted butter
125g caster sugar
125g ground almonds
3 medium free-range eggs
2 tbsp rum

TO FINISH
apricot jam warmed with a
    little water
1 tbsp sliced almonds

Beignets à la crème

CREAM FRITTERS

Everyone likes fritters or doughnuts once in a while and these are a real sweet temptation. They are rich though, so best for occasional consumption only. The fruit tempers the richness well and can be varied according to the season and your preference.

First make the cream filling. Whisk the sugar, egg and egg yolks together in a bowl, then whisk in the flour. Bring the milk to the boil in a pan with the strips of peel and pour this on to the egg mixture. Whisk well, then pour everything back into the pan and heat until boiling. It will become very thick so keep whisking to prevent the mixture sticking or burning. Line a shallow baking tray, measuring about 30 x 20cm, with cling film. Remove the orange peel from the mixture and spread it out on the lined tray. Cover and chill for about 2–3 hours until set.

To make the raspberry coulis for the garnish, blitz the raspberries with the 100g sugar and lemon juice to taste. Pass through a fine sieve.

Cut the sticks of rhubarb into pieces of about 4cm long. Melt the 80g of caster sugar in the grenadine – you may need to add a tablespoon of water. Place the rhubarb pieces in a wide pan so that they fit snugly and add the liquid. Simmer for 2–3 minutes, then carefully flip them over. Make sure not to overcook the rhubarb – it should retain a little bite.

Make the batter at the last moment by mixing the dry ingredients in a bowl, then whisking in the water. Pour the oil into a large pan or a deep-fat fryer and heat to 180°C.

Take a spoonful of the cream mixture and dip it into the batter, then carefully place it into the hot frying oil. Cook just a few beignets at a time, moving them around in the oil with a slotted spoon, for 30 seconds to a minute until golden and crisp. Take care not to overcrowd the pan.

Drain the beignets on kitchen paper and serve them warm with the raspberry coulis and poached rhubarb. Sprinkle with a little icing sugar before serving.

SERVES 6

CREAM FILLING
60g caster sugar
1 free-range egg
4 free-range egg yolks
80g plain flour
500ml milk
thinly pared peel of
    2 oranges, cut into
    fine strips

GARNISH
400g raspberries
100g sugar
juice of ½ lemon
4 sticks of rhubarb
80g caster sugar
1 tbsp grenadine syrup
1 tsp icing sugar, for serving

BATTER
60g cornflour
185g plain flour
1 tsp baking powder
475ml carbonated water
2 litres vegetable oil, for
    deep-frying

Panna cotta au babeurre et figues

BUTTERMILK PANNA COTTA WITH FIGS

This is a very lightly set panna cotta that can't be turned
out so make it in pretty glass bowls for serving. The
panna cottas are topped with pistachio crumbs made
from a shortbread-like mixture and decorated with
tuiles and figs. Make all the trimmings to create a really
special dessert or just garnish with figs – up to you.
It will always be a delight.

To make the panna cottas, pour the cream into a pan and add the fig leaves,
vanilla pods and sugar. Bring this to the boil, then whisk in the gelatine and
pour in the buttermilk. Stir, then strain through a sieve into 12 glass bowls
and leave in the fridge to set for 8 hours.

For the tuiles, heat all the ingredients except the bicarbonate in a pan to
140°C or until the mixture starts to turn golden. Stir in the bicarbonate of
soda, then pour the mixture into a deep dish lined with a silicone baking
mat or non-stick baking parchment. Be very careful as it will spit and
splash. Leave this to cool and set.

Preheat the oven to 200°C/Fan 180°C/Gas 6. Blitz the cooled honeycomb to
a powder in a food processor, then sprinkle it on to a silicone baking mat or
a baking tray lined with non-stick baking parchment and put it in the oven
for a couple of minutes until melted. Cut into whatever shapes you like.

For the pistachio crumbs, mix the flour, ground almonds and sugar together.
Using your fingertips, gently work in the butter and pistachios – the mixture
should just come together into a paste so don't overwork it. Wrap it in cling
film and chill for an hour.

Preheat the oven to 180°C/Fan 160°C/Gas 4. Roll out the pistachio paste to
about 0.5–1cm thick and place it on a baking tray. Prick it with a fork and
cook for about 25 minutes. Leave to cool, then break up into crumbs. Toss
the figs in the oil and pepper, then cut into bite-sized pieces.

When the panna cottas are set, serve them topped with pistachio crumbs
and a couple of tuiles and figs.

SERVES 12

PANNA COTTA
500ml double cream
4 fig leaves
2 vanilla pods, split
200g caster sugar
4 leaves of gelatine (softened
in cold water and
squeezed)
500ml buttermilk

HONEYCOMB TUILES
140g caster sugar
25g honey
60g glucose
30g water
8g bicarbonate of soda

PISTACHIO CRUMBS
60g plain flour
25g ground almonds
50g caster sugar
35g unsalted butter, melted
40g pistachio nuts, finely
chopped

DRESSED FIGS
4 figs, cut into quarters
1 tbsp extra virgin olive oil
black pepper

Babas au Calvados

CALVADOS BABAS

One of the many great things about this recipe is that nearly all the work can be done well in advance, leaving just the final glaze and assembly when you're ready to eat. The traditional baba is served with rum and I remember as an apprentice not being allowed to make these delicious cakes for fear that I would get inebriated. This version uses Calvados, another potent spirit, and just as good. If serving kids, leave the Calvados out of the syrup and let the adults help themselves. You can make babas in any shape, such as rings, but I like to use little moulds of about 4 x 3cm.

Dissolve the yeast in the milk in a food mixer bowl. Add the flour, honey, salt and eggs and knead with the dough hook attachment for 5 minutes. Scrape down the edges, add the butter and continue to work the dough until the butter has been incorporated. Cover and leave to rise for 45 minutes.

Preheat the oven to 200°C/Fan 180°C/Gas 6. Butter your moulds, unless they are non-stick silicone ones. Knock back the dough, then half fill the baba moulds with it. Leave them to rise again for 30 minutes, then bake in the preheated oven until golden and fully cooked – this should take about 20 minutes. Take the babas out of the moulds and leave to cool on a rack

To make the compote, peel and roughly chop the apples. Put them in a pan with the sugar and a splash of water, then bring to a simmer. Mash the apples as they cook until you have a soft compote. Leave to cool until needed.

To make the syrup, put the lemon grass in a small pan with the apple juice, lime juice and sugar. Bring to the boil and then pass through a fine sieve. Add Calvados to taste. Dunk the babas in the lukewarm syrup until swollen, plump and completely soaked. The syrup shouldn't be too hot or the babas may crack, but if it is too cold, the babas will not soak as well. Place them on a wire rack to drain, then refrigerate until needed.

Just before serving, make the glaze. Pour the apple juice into a pan, add the sugar and boil until the sugar has melted. Mix the cornflour and lemon juice, then whisk this into the boiling apple juice to thicken. Brush the babas with the glaze to give them a lovely sheen, then serve on a bed of apple compote. Top with Chantilly cream and apple crisps if you like.

MAKES 8 BABAS

8g fresh yeast

2 tbsp milk

200g flour

10g clear honey

10g salt

3 medium free-range eggs

75g softened, unsalted butter, plus extra for greasing

Chantilly cream, for serving (see page 340)

apple crisps, for serving (see page 338)

APPLE COMPOTE

4 eating apples (Braeburns or Cox)

4 tbsp sugar

SYRUP

2 sticks of lemon grass, roughly chopped

250ml pure apple juice

juice of 2 limes

100g brown sugar

good splash of Calvados

GLAZE

250ml fresh (cloudy) apple juice

25g caster sugar

20g cornflour

25ml lemon juice

Marquise au chocolat

CHOCOLATE MARQUISE

This almost forgotten French classic is a wonderful
layered construction of biscuit and flavoured ganache.
It's perfect for a special occasion as you can make it in
advance and keep it in the fridge ready to slice when
you want. There are many variations but this recipe,
with the retro touch of After Eight mints, was on the
menu at Le Gavroche back in the early days and is just
as popular when it makes an appearance now. The
quantities here make a little more biscuit than you
need to allow for trimmings and any mishaps – no
hardship to finish them up though.

First make the biscuit. Preheat the oven to 200°C/Fan 180°C/Gas 6. Line a
baking tray with lightly buttered and floured greaseproof paper. Whisk the
egg whites until frothy, then add 180g of the sugar and continue to whisk
until firm. Fold in the ground almonds, remaining sugar and milk powder.
Spread the mixture on to the lined baking tray to a thickness of 5mm and
sprinkle with the hazelnuts. Cook in the preheated oven for 20 minutes or
until just set. Leave to cool, then cut into 3 neat strips measuring 20 x 9cm.

Melt the chocolate in a bowl over barely simmering water – don't let it get
too hot. Whip the cream to soft peaks. Pour half the melted chocolate on to
the cream and mix with a whisk, then gently add the remaining chocolate.
Divide this into 3 and flavour one with rum, one with crème de menthe and
leave the third plain. Leave until cool and semi-set to the consistency of
thick mayonnaise – it needs to be firm enough to build your marquise.

Cut a piece of card measuring 20 x 12cm and cover it with foil – this will be
your base for the marquise. Place a strip of biscuit on the base, spread it with
a layer of rum ganache, then sprinkle on the chopped ginger. Add another
strip of biscuit, spread with the crème de menthe ganache and arrange the
After Eights on top. Add the third biscuit, then spread the plain ganache
over the top and sides and smooth with a palette knife. Place the marquise
in the fridge to set for at least an hour.

When you're ready to serve, dip a knife in hot water and cut the marquise
into slices of about 2cm thick.

SERVES 12

BISCUIT
butter, for greasing
flour, for dusting
5 free-range egg whites
255g caster sugar
75g ground almonds
12g milk powder
2 tbsp chopped hazelnuts

GANACHE
750g extra bitter chocolate
750ml double cream
30ml dark rum
30ml crème de menthe
60g crystallised ginger,
    coarsely chopped
18 After Eight mints

Feuilleté aux raisins et Kirsch

PUFF PASTRY WITH GRAPES AND KIRSCH

This is an impressive-looking dessert, but can be made with shop-bought puff pastry and most of the work can be done in advance. The light, crisp feuilleté – puff pastry circles – are slightly hollowed out which makes them lighter, and the Kirsch-soaked grapes are mouth-wateringly good. The longer they are soaked the better they are. Put it all together with the warm sabayon sauce at the last minute and serve right away.

SERVES 4

icing sugar, for dusting
360g all-butter puff pastry
320g seedless white grapes
100ml Kirsch
100g caster sugar
80ml water
6 medium free-range
   egg yolks

Dust your work surface with icing sugar and roll out the pastry to a thickness of 5mm. Cut out 8 circles and place these on a moistened, non-stick baking tray – brushing the baking tray with water stops the pastry shrinking. Leave the pastry to rest in the fridge for at least 20 minutes.

Meanwhile, peel the grapes with a small knife or a teaspoon, and put them in the Kirsch to marinate. Make a sugar syrup by boiling the caster sugar with the 80ml of water. Preheat the oven to 230°C/Fan 210°C/Gas 8.

Dust the puff pastry circles with a little more icing sugar and put them in the preheated oven for 5 minutes. Turn the heat down to 180°C/Fan 160°C/Gas 4 and cook for another 10 minutes, until golden brown and puffed up. Place on a wire rack to cool.

Drain the grapes, reserving the Kirsch. Put them in a pan with half the sugar syrup and warm through over a low heat.

To make the sabayon, put the egg yolks, Kirsch (collected from the grapes) and the rest of the sugar syrup in a bowl over a pan of simmering water. Whisk over a low heat until you have a smooth rich sauce and the whisk leaves a trail when lifted.

Using the point of a knife, carefully hollow out the pastry circles – working from the top of 4 of them and from the bottom of the other 4 – removing any pastry that may not have fully cooked. Place the 4 bases on a plate, fill with the warmed grapes and sabayon, and pop the lids on top. Serve at once.

Kouign-amann

LAYERED BUTTER YEAST CAKE

A true Brittany classic, this yeast cake has many
variations but all are laden with local butter. The name
comes from the local dialect – *kouign*, meaning cake
and *amann*, meaning butter. This is at its best when
freshly baked and needs nothing more than a cup of
milky coffee or a glass of local sweet cider.

SERVES 8

15g fresh yeast
180ml tepid water
275g plain flour, plus
    extra for dusting
pinch of sea salt
110g salted butter
200g caster sugar

Dissolve the yeast in the water, add the flour and salt, then begin to knead
until you have a smooth dough. It may seem a little sticky but that's fine.
Cover the dough and leave it to rise for an hour.

Roll the dough out on a floured surface to make a rectangle of about 30cm
long and 20cm wide. Cut the butter into 2cm cubes and scatter them down
the middle of the rectangle with 50g of the sugar. Fold the pastry over,
sprinkle on another 50g of sugar, then fold again to form what is almost
a square.

Wrap the dough in cling film and refrigerate for 45 minutes. Repeat the
rolling process, adding another 50g of sugar at each fold. Leave the dough
to rest for 30 minutes, then roll it out into a 20cm circle and place it in a flan
or pie dish.

Leave to rise again for 30 minutes, then sprinkle over a little more sugar
and a couple of extra knobs of salted butter if feeling particularly indulgent.
Preheat the oven to 220°C/Fan 200°C/Gas 7.

Place the dish in the hot oven for 20 minutes, then turn the temperature
down to 200°C/Fan 180°C/Gas 6 for a further 20 minutes. Eat the cake while
it is still warm.

Tarte Bressane

SUGAR TART

Also known as tarte au sucre, this is a delicious yeasty
brioche-like tart covered in cream and sugar from the
Bresse region of France (north of Lyon). There are
many variations, including some with pink pralines,
but this is the one that I like the most. Delicious on its
own or with some fruit compote and best served warm.

Dissolve the yeast in the milk and place in the bowl of a food mixer. Add the
flour, sugar, salt and eggs and knead with the dough hook attachment until
you have an elastic dough. Add the melted butter and continue to work for at
least 5 minutes, scraping down the mixture from the edges when necessary.
Cover and leave to rise for 1 hour. Lightly butter a 20cm flan dish.

Knock back the dough to release the gases, then transfer it to the flan dish.
Spread the dough out, then cover with cling film and leave to rise again –
this time for just 20 minutes. Preheat the oven to 220°C/Fan 200°C/Gas 7.

Place the tart in the preheated oven for 10 minutes. Split the vanilla pod and
scrape out the seeds, then mix them into the crème fraiche. Take the tart out
of the oven and spread the crème fraiche over the top. Quickly sprinkle on
the brown sugar and return the tart to the oven for a further 20 minutes or
until fully cooked and brown on top.

SERVES 6

10g fresh yeast
10ml warm milk
250g plain flour
50g caster sugar
5g salt
3 medium free-range eggs
80g unsalted butter, melted,
   plus extra for greasing

TOPPING

1 vanilla pod
170g crème fraiche
60g brown sugar

Coupe de pêche rose chéri

PEACHES WITH CHERRIES AND CREAM

Best served in fancy glasses with some wafers or crisp biscuits, this luscious peach confection is as old as the famous peach Melba, but is flavoured with cherries instead of raspberries.

Bring a pan of water to the boil, add the peaches and blanch them for a couple of minutes. Refresh them in iced water, then peel off the skins.

Make a sugar syrup by boiling 600g of the caster sugar with 1 litre of water for 5 minutes. Carefully add the peaches to the boiling syrup and simmer for 20 minutes, then leave to cool.

Put the cherries in a wide saucepan with the remaining 150g of caster sugar and the lemon juice and bring to the boil. Add the redcurrant jelly and continue to cook until the jelly has melted, then leave to cool.

Whisk the cream with the icing sugar until stiff. Spoon some cherries and their sauce into each glass. Cut the peaches in half, remove the stones and fill the cavities with ice cream. Place the peaches on top of the cherries and pipe the whipped cream on top.

SERVES 6

6 yellow peaches
750g caster sugar
1 litre water
300g dark cherries, stoned
juice of 1 lemon
150g redcurrant jelly
250ml whipping cream,
    whipped
80g icing sugar
vanilla ice cream

Soufflé aux fraises

STRAWBERRY CRUMBLE SOUFFLÉ

Strawberries go beautifully with Kirsch and these little soufflés are gorgeous. Make them in individual ramekins of about 8 x 6cm and serve them with some clotted cream if you like.

Wash and hull the strawberries, then place them in a pan with the demerara sugar, lemon juice and 2 tablespoons of water. Bring to a simmer, stir gently and cook until tender. Remove 1 or 2 strawberries per person to serve as a garnish and douse them with the Kirsch.

Put the rest of the strawberries in a food processor with the cooking juices and blitz them to a purée. Pass the purée through a fine sieve into a clean saucepan. Mix the cornflour with 2 tablespoons of water to make a paste and add this to the purée. Bring to the boil, stirring constantly to avoid any lumps. Leave the mixture to cool, but do not refrigerate.

To make the crumble topping, mix all the ingredients together and spread the mixture over a non-stick baking tray. Preheat the oven to 220°C/Fan 200°C/Gas 7. Toast the crumble for a few minutes, then remove and turn the oven down to 200°C/Fan 180°C/Gas 6.

Whisk the egg whites until frothy, then add the 80g of caster sugar and continue to whisk until stiff peaks form. Take a third of the egg whites and beat them into the cooled purée, then gently fold in the rest of the egg whites. Butter your ramekins thoroughly and coat the insides with sugar. Always work upwards when buttering soufflé dishes as this helps the soufflés rise.

Half fill the ramekins with the strawberry mixture, then add the reserved strawberries and Kirsch. Fill the ramekins to the top, level with a palette knife and place them in the preheated oven for 8 minutes. Sprinkle on some crumble topping and continue to cook for a further 2–3 minutes. Serve with a spoonful of clotted cream if you like.

SERVES 8

600g strawberries
4 tbsp demerara sugar
juice of 1 lemon
2 tbsp Kirsch
2 tbsp cornflour
10 free-range egg whites
80g caster sugar, plus extra
    for dusting
unsalted butter, for greasing
clotted cream, for serving
    (optional)

CRUMBLE TOPPING

1 tbsp chopped pistachios
1 tbsp nibbed almonds
1 tbsp demerara sugar
1 tbsp rolled oats
1 tbsp desiccated coconut

La découverte d'un mets nouveau
fait plus pour le bonheur du genre
humain que la découverte d'une étoile

The discovery of a new dish confers
more happiness on humanity, than the
discovery of a new star

JEAN ANTHELME BRILLAT-SAVARIN

Riz impératrice

EMPRESS RICE PUDDING

This old-fashioned rice dessert is timeless in my view
and is a long way away from the stodgy rice pudding
that's often passed off as a classic. There's quite a bit of
work involved but it's well worth it.

First soak the dried fruit. Make a sugar syrup by boiling 250ml of water with
the 100g sugar, then add the fruit, pistachios and a splosh of Kirsch to taste.
Leave for a couple of hours or overnight.

Put the rice in a pan and cover with plenty of water. Bring it to the boil and
cook for 5 minutes, then drain. Tip the rice back into the pan with the milk,
split vanilla pod and 50g of sugar. Simmer until all the liquid has been
absorbed, then cover and leave to cool.

To make the crème anglaise, whisk the egg yolks and sugar in a bowl. Bring
the milk to the boil, pour it on to the eggs and sugar and mix well. Return the
mixture to the pan and cook gently until thickened. Do not let it boil or the
eggs will scramble.

Put the gelatine in a dish of cold water to soften, then squeeze dry and add it
to the hot crème anglaise. Pass the mixture through a sieve – set the vanilla
pod aside to use as decoration if you like. When the crème is cool, add it to
the rice mix, then fold in the whipped cream.

Lightly oil a mould such as 1.5-litre pudding basin. Pour in half the rice
mixture, add some of the drained, soaked fruit (reserving the rest and the
syrup), then cover with the remaining mixture.

Leave the pudding in the fridge to set overnight, then decorate with a few
of the soaked fruits. Serve with the rest of the fruit and syrup.

SERVES 10–12

120g round pudding rice
360ml milk
1 vanilla pod, split
50g caster sugar

CRÈME ANGLAISE

4 medium free-range egg
   yolks
100g caster sugar
375ml milk
3 gelatine leaves
250ml whipping cream,
   whipped
vegetable oil, for greasing

DRIED FRUIT

250ml water
100g caster sugar
180g mixed dried fruit
   (apricots, prunes,
   cherries, to taste)
2 tbsp pistachio nuts
Kirsch, to taste

Millefeuille à la mangue et grenade

MILLEFEUILLE WITH MANGO AND POMEGRANATE

The seasoning of the mango is vital to this dessert.
In the tropics, mangoes and pineapples are often served
sprinkled with pepper or chilli – both a perfect foil for
the fragrant flowery sweetness of these fruits. For this
recipe you need mangoes that are ripe enough to taste
good but not so ripe that you can't slice them neatly. If
you can't manage the mango curls, don't worry – cut
your mangoes into matchsticks and the millefeuille will
still taste delicious.

Roll out the puff pastry on a lightly floured surface to form a rectangle,
2.5mm thick – that's about the thickness of a 2 pence coin. Place the pastry
on a baking tray and leave in the fridge to rest for 30 minutes.

Preheat the oven to 220°C/Fan 200°C/Gas 7. Prick the pastry at intervals
with a fork to prevent it from shrinking as it cooks. Place a sheet of
greaseproof paper on top, followed by another baking tray to keep the
pastry flat. Bake for 10 minutes, then remove the tray and paper. Turn the
oven temperature down to 200°C/Fan 180°C/Gas 6 and cook the pastry for
another 20 minutes or until crisp and cooked through. Remove from the
oven and carefully slip the pastry on to a wire rack to cool. Cut the pastry
into 12 rectangles, each 8 x 4cm.

To make the crème pâtissière, whisk the eggs with the sugar in a bowl and
add the flour. Bring the milk to the boil and pour it into the bowl, mixing
well. Tip the mixture back into the saucepan and bring it to the boil,
whisking constantly. Remove from the heat as soon as it boils and dust the
surface with a little icing sugar to avoid a crust or skin forming. Once the
crème is completely cold, fold in the whipped cream.

Skin the mangoes, slice them and season with the lime zest, half the lime
juice and the piment d'Espelette. Roll the slices into curls as neatly as you
can. To make the sauce, blitz all the mango trimmings with the caster sugar
and the rest of the lime juice until smooth.

To assemble, take a pastry rectangle and pipe a little crème pâtissière over it.
Add some mango curls, pomegranate seeds and then repeat, finishing with a
layer of pastry. Dust with icing sugar or add some spun sugar or tiny brandy
snaps if you like. Serve with the mango sauce.

SERVES 4

250g all-butter puff pastry
plain flour, for rolling
6 ripe mangoes
 grated zest of 1 lime and
  juice of 2
1 tsp ground piment
  d'Espelette (chilli
  powder)
 60g caster sugar
seeds from 1 fresh
  pomegranate
icing sugar, for dusting

CRÈME PÂTISSIÈRE

3 medium free-range egg
  yolks
60g caster sugar
25g flour
200ml milk
100ml double cream,
  whipped

Fraises Sarah Bernhardt

STRAWBERRIES SARAH BERNHARDT

I couldn't write a book of French classics without doffing my chef's hat to this wonderful dessert, created by Escoffier for the famous actress of the day. You can serve this in one large bowl but it looks wonderfully retro in individual glasses.

To make the pineapple sorbet, peel the pineapple and dice the flesh. Put this in a pan with the sugar, glucose and lemon juice and bring it to the boil, then blitz until smooth in a food processor. Freeze in an ice-cream machine. Alternatively, you can spoon the mixture into a tray, cover and leave in the freezer to set, mixing every 30 minutes until smooth.

To make the mousse, whisk the yolks and sugar together in a bowl. Bring the milk to the boil with the orange peel, then pour this on to the yolks and mix well. Tip the mixture back into the pan and cook carefully until it thickens. Place the gelatine in a saucer of cold water until it softens, then squeeze out the excess water. Add the softened gelatine and the Curaçao to the egg mixture, then pass through a fine sieve. Leave to cool and when almost set fold in the whipped cream. Refrigerate until firm.

Hull the strawberries and cut them in half or quarters if large. Douse with the brandy and Curaçao, then cover and refrigerate for at least an hour.

To serve, spoon some of the pineapple sorbet into each dish followed by the strawberries and juices, then top with some Curaçao mousse. Decorate with some spun sugar if you like.

To make spun sugar, melt 200 grams of caster sugar in a frying pan until it turns golden brown – watch it carefully and don't let it burn. Remove the pan from the heat and use a fork to flick the sugar back and forth over a greased wooden spoon or ladle to make a fragile cage.

SERVES 6

500g strawberries
2 tbsp brandy
4 tbsp Curaçao

PINEAPPLE SORBET
1 sweet, golden pineapple
a third of the pineapple's peeled weight in caster sugar
2 tbsp liquid glucose
1 lemon juice

CURAÇAO MOUSSE
3 medium free-range egg yolks
80g caster sugar
250ml milk
2 thinly pared strips of orange peel
2 gelatine leaves
4 tbsp Curaçao
100ml whipping cream, whipped

Galette serpentine

ALMOND PUFF PASTRY

This is a lost version of the famous pithiviers — a different shape but just as delicious. It's best served warm from the oven and perfect for tea.

To make the almond cream, beat the butter until it's smooth and creamy, then whisk in the ground almonds and icing sugar. Beat in the eggs, one at a time, and once they are all incorporated, add the rum.

Roll out the puff pastry to a strip measuring about 13cm wide and 50cm long. Trim the edges so the strip is perfectly straight. Pipe the almond cream down the middle of the strip, then lightly brush one edge with beaten egg and fold over to seal. Make sure there are no air pockets.

Preheat the oven to 220°C/Fan 200°C/Gas 7. Make little cuts 5mm apart all the way along the sealed edge of the strip. Arrange the strip in a spiral on a non-stick baking sheet, with the cut edge facing out. Brush with beaten egg and cook for 10 minutes, then turn down the oven to 200°C/Fan 180°C/Gas 6 for another 20 minutes or until the galette is cooked through. Take the galette out of the oven and carefully slide it on to a wire rack to cool slightly before serving.

SERVES 10

400g all-butter puff pastry
2 free-range egg yolks,
   beaten, for brushing

ALMOND CREAM
160g soft unsalted butter
160g ground almonds
160g icing sugar
3 medium free-range eggs
1 tbsp rum

Charlotte aux poires

PEAR CHARLOTTE

This is a boozy delight and takes me back to my days as an apprentice when charlottes were in fashion. All kinds of flavours and perfumes were used but my all-time favourite is this pear version. I use canned pears, which may come as a surprise but they work beautifully.

You will need a charlotte mould or a loose-based 20cm cake tin. First make the biscuit for lining the mould. Separate the eggs and whisk the yolks with 160g of the caster sugar until pale. Whisk the whites until frothy, add the remaining caster sugar and whisk again until firm. Gently fold this into the yolk mixture. Once nearly all the egg white is incorporated, fold in the flour – take care not to over mix.

Put the biscuit mixture in a piping bag. Pipe a circle of dots on to a non-stick baking mat. The circle should be the same diameter as the mould and the dots should be touching. Next pipe another circle in a spiral on to another mat to form the base of the charlotte. Pipe the rest of the mixture in diagonal strips on to a separate non-stick baking mat, piping the strips close together so they touch. Dust with icing sugar and bake all the biscuit at 210°C/Fan 190°C/Gas 6½ for 12 minutes or until cooked. Leave to cool.

Set the circles aside. Cut out sections of the strips the same depth as the mould to line the sides. Line the base of your mould with the biscuit circle, then line the sides with sections of the strips, making sure there are no gaps. Moisten with a little of the pear syrup and liqueur.

Now make the bavarois mixture. Place the gelatine in iced water to soften. Whisk the yolks and caster sugar in a bowl until pale. Pour the pear syrup into a saucepan, then add the milk powder and vanilla pod and bring to the boil. Pour the boiling pear milk on to the yolks, mix well, then tip back into the pan and cook until it's thickened and coats the back of a spoon. Once the mixture reaches 82°C (check with a thermometer) remove from the heat and add the drained, squeezed gelatine. Pass through a fine sieve and leave to cool a little before adding the pear liqueur. Cover with cling film and chill.

Once the mixture is cold and semi-set, fold in the whipped cream. Pour half the mixture into the lined mould, add plenty of chopped pear, then pour on the rest of the bavarois. Leave to cool overnight, then top with the circle of biscuit dots and serve. This also freezes well so can be made in advance.

SERVES 12

4 gelatine leaves (bronze)
6 medium free-range egg yolks
50g caster sugar
250ml pear syrup from the can
25g milk powder
1 vanilla pod, split
190ml poire William liqueur
375ml whipping cream, whipped
240g canned pears, chopped

BISCUIT CUILLÈRE

9 medium free-range eggs
280g caster sugar
270g plain flour
45g icing sugar, for dusting

Tarte au chocolat

WARM BITTER CHOCOLATE TART

Use the best chocolate you can get for making this tart,
as it really is worth it. And yes, it does contain a lot of
butter but it is very special. It's great for a party as you
can make it the day before and keep it in the fridge, but
do warm it through gently and serve it tepid.

To make the pastry, cut the butter into small pieces and leave it to soften
at room temperature. Sift the flour and salt, place them on the work
surface and make a well in the centre. Add the butter and sugar and gently
work together with your fingertips. Add the egg yolk and gradually draw
in the flour, adding drops of water as you go. When all the flour has been
incorporated, shape the dough into a ball, but do not overwork it. Wrap the
pastry in cling film and refrigerate for at least 2 hours before using.

To make the bitter orange sauce, boil the orange juice and sugar until
reduced by three-quarters. Add the marmalade, stir until it has melted,
then pass the sauce through a fine sieve. Leave to cool.

Preheat the oven to 180°C/Fan 160°C/Gas 4. Roll out the pastry and use it
to line a 26cm flan tin. Cover the base of the pastry with greaseproof paper
and add some dried beans, then bake for 20 minutes. Remove the beans and
paper and return the pastry to the oven for 5 minutes to cook completely.
Turn the oven down to 140°C/Fan 120°C/Gas 1.

Whisk the whole eggs, yolks and sugar with an electric mixer at full speed for
5 minutes, or until pale and frothy. Melt the chocolate and butter in a bowl
set over a pan of simmering water, then fold into the egg mixture. Pour this
on to the pastry base, place the tart in the oven immediately and bake for 15
minutes. Remove and leave to cool to tepid before serving with bitter orange
sauce and some ice cream (see pages 294–296).

SERVES 8

3 free-range eggs

4 free-range egg yolks

175g caster sugar

375g bitter chocolate
(70% cocoa solids),
roughly chopped

250g unsalted butter, cubed

SWEET PASTRY

80g unsalted butter

130g plain flour, plus extra
for dusting

pinch of salt

30g sugar

1 free-range egg yolk

1 tbsp water

BITTER ORANGE SAUCE

200ml fresh orange juice

100g caster sugar

2 tbsp bitter orange
marmalade

Poires pochées aux amandes et chocolat

POACHED PEARS WITH CHOCOLATE ALMOND SAUCE

Pears and chocolate are a fabulous combination and one of my favourites. Serve these pears warm with the chocolate sauce and, if feeling particularly indulgent, some whipped cream.

Put the sugar, scraped vanilla pod and seeds with the water in a pan and bring to the boil. Peel the pears and remove their cores from the base, then place them in the simmering syrup. Cover with greaseproof paper and cook until a knife pierces the pear easily – the exact time will depend on the ripeness of the pear. Leave the pears in the syrup to cool slightly while you make the sauce.

To make the sauce, boil the water with the cocoa powder and sugar, while whisking vigorously. Take the pan off the heat and whisk in the butter and chocolate, then add the almonds. Serve with the poached pears.

SERVES 4

350g caster sugar
1 vanilla pod, split and
    seeds scraped out
500ml water
4 pears (Williams or
    similar)
whipped cream (optional)

CHOCOLATE ALMOND SAUCE

250ml water
60g unsweetened cocoa
    powder
120g caster sugar
30g unsalted butter
40g bitter chocolate, broken
    into pieces
60g almonds, toasted and
    chopped

On doit aimer soit ce qu'on va manger, soit la personne pour laquelle on cuisine. Ensuite, vous devez vous donner à la cuisine – la cuisine est un acte d'amour

You have to love either what you are going to eat, or the person you are cooking for. Then you have to give yourself up to the cooking – cooking is an act of love

ALAIN CHAPEL

Petits pots de crème

LITTLE CREAM POTS

Like crème brûleè and crème caramel, these little
desserts are set custards and are baked in individual
pots, traditionally with their own lids. If you do not
have pots with lids you can cover the custards with foil,
making a little hole to allow steam to escape. I find that
little glass yoghurt pots are ideal.

SERVES 8

3 free-range eggs
4 free-range egg yolks
100g caster sugar
220ml milk
220ml single cream
1 vanilla pod, split and seeds
   scraped out

Preheat the oven to 180°C/Fan 160°C/Gas 4. Whisk the eggs and yolks with
the sugar until pale. Bring the milk and cream to the boil with the vanilla
pod and seeds, then pour this on to the egg mixture and whisk well. Pass the
custard through a sieve and pour it into little pots or cups. Carefully remove
all the froth from the tops and put on the lids or foil. Make a little hole in the
foil tops, if using.

Place the pots in an ovenproof dish and pour in enough hot water to reach
about a third of the way up the sides of the dish. Bake in the oven for about
30 minutes or until set, depending on the size. Smaller pots won't take quite
as long. Traditionally these simple little sweets are served just as they are,
but if you want to dress them up, pipe a little rosette of Chantilly cream (see
page 340) on top.

PETITS POTS DE CRÈME AU CHOCOLAT

For a chocolate version, stir 170g of bitter chocolate (70% cocoa solids) into
the boiling milk and cream.

If you would like to make some of each type, divide the mixture in half and
add just 85g of chocolate to one half.

Iles flottantes et compote de fraises

FLOATING ISLANDS WITH STRAWBERRY COMPOTE

Floating islands, without the strawberries, is a
traditional Easter dessert in France and one my mother
always used to make. But it is so good I love to eat it at
any time of year and with strawberry compote it has
become a summertime favourite of Le Gavroche clients.

SERVES 4

500g strawberries, washed
    and hulled
100g sugar, or to taste
6 free-range egg whites
640g caster sugar

CRÈME ANGLAISE
500ml milk
1 vanilla pod, split
6 free-range egg yolks
120g caster sugar

To make the strawberry compote, tip the washed and hulled strawberries
into a pan and sprinkle them with a little sugar. The exact amount of
sugar depends on the sweetness of the berries. Bring this to the boil, then
immediately take off the heat, cover and leave to cool.

To make the crème anglaise, bring the milk to the boil with the vanilla pod.
Remove the pan from the heat, cover and leave to infuse for 10 minutes.
Beat the egg yolks with the sugar until thick and creamy. Bring the milk
back to the boil and pour it on to the yolk mixture, whisking continuously.
Pour the mixture back into the saucepan and cook over a low heat, stirring
continuously with a spatula, until the custard thickens slightly.

Beat the egg whites with a whisk until frothy, then add 340g of the caster
sugar. Continue to whisk until the meringue is firm and smooth.

Bring a large pan of water, sweetened with 2 tablespoons of the caster sugar,
to simmering point. Using a big kitchen spoon dipped in cold water, scoop
out a big island of meringue and plunge the spoon into the simmering
water. The island should come off the spoon into the water and poach in this
liquid, flipping it over after 3–4 minutes to cook on both sides. Continue
until all the egg whites are used.

Once cooked, gently take the islands out of the liquid with a slotted spoon
and place them on a rack to cool and drain. When they're cold, heat the rest
of the caster sugar in a heavy pan until liquid and golden, then pour this
caramel over the top of each island.

To serve, place some compote in each bowl, followed by crème anglaise
flavoured with vanilla, and finally the caramel-coated floating islands.

Gâteau de riz au bain marie

BATH PUDDING

This is a recipe that dates back to the mid 1700s and it was probably named Bath pudding because it was cooked in a bath of water rather than after the town. Lovely served with some warm fruit compote.

Grind the rice in a food processor until it is the texture of fine semolina. Mix a little of the milk with the ground rice and a pinch of salt to make a paste.

Bring the rest of the milk and cream to the boil, with the thinly pared lemon peel. Pour this on to the rice paste and stir well, then tip it all back into the pan and bring to the boil. Leave to cool for about 10 minutes, then remove the peel.

Butter a 750ml jelly mould or pudding basin. Whisk the whole eggs, yolk, sugar and grated lemon zest in a large bowl, then stir in the rice mixture and mix well. Pour the mixture into the buttered mould or basin and cover with foil. Place the bowl in a saucepan and add hot water to come about halfway up the sides. Bring the water to the boil, then simmer gently for 1½ hours or until the pudding is set. Leave to cool for a few moments before turning out.

Brush with some melted jam and serve with a warm fruit compote.

SERVES 6—8

60g round pudding rice
450ml milk
1 pinch of salt
50ml double cream
thinly pared peel of ½ lemon
unsalted butter, for greasing
2 free-range eggs
1 free-range egg yolk
60g sugar
finely grated zest of ½ lemon
raspberry jam, melted

Clafoutis aux pruneaux

PRUNE CLAFOUTIS

A family favourite and a dish that my grandma used to cook. Cherry clafoutis is the classic version but when cherries are not in season, make a clafoutis with prunes instead. It's equally delicious and even better if you soak the prunes in a good splosh of brandy the day before making the clafoutis.

Lightly butter a 23cm flan dish and preheat the oven to 180°C/Fan 160°C/Gas 4. Put the prunes in the dish.

Whisk the eggs and sugar in a bowl until light and pale in colour. Add the scrapings of the vanilla pod and the sifted flour, then slowly pour in the milk without over whisking and add the melted butter. Pass the mixture through a fine sieve, then pour it into the dish over the prunes. Cook the clafoutis for 30 minutes or until puffed up and set.

SERVES 6—8

30g unsalted butter, melted, plus extra for greasing
30 prunes, stoned
3 free-range eggs
60g caster sugar
1 vanilla pod, split and seeds scraped out
25g plain flour, sifted
350ml milk

Glace à la vanille

VANILLA ICE CREAM

Bring the milk to the boil with the vanilla pods, then remove the pan from the heat, cover and leave to infuse for 10 minutes.

Beat the egg yolks with the sugar until thick and creamy. Bring the milk back to the boil and pour it on to the yolk mixture, whisking continuously. Pour the mixture back into the saucepan and cook over a low heat, stirring constantly with a spatula until the custard thickens slightly. Stir in the vanilla extract and pass through a fine sieve. Chill, then churn in an ice-cream machine until frozen.

SERVES 12

1 litre full-fat milk
4 vanilla pods, split
12 free-range egg yolks
250g caster sugar
2 tsp vanilla extract

Glace aux pruneaux et Armagnac

PRUNE AND ARMAGNAC ICE CREAM

Prepare the prunes a week ahead. Remove the stones and put the prunes in a bowl, then sprinkle them with sugar and douse with the Armagnac. Cover tightly and refrigerate.

When you're ready to make the ice cream, drain the prunes and add the liquid to the ice cream mix and churn as above. Just before serving, remove the ice cream from the freezer and leave until it becomes pliable, then fold in the roughly chopped prunes.

SERVES 12

6 Agen prunes
2 tbsp demerara sugar
120ml Armagnac
1 quantity of vanilla ice
   cream (see above)

Glace au beurre noisette

BROWN BUTTER ICE CREAM

Heat the sugar in a pan until brown and caramelised. Add the water, milk and cream, and bring to the boil – take care when adding the liquid to the hot sugar, as it may bubble up fiercely.

Heat the butter in a separate pan until it starts to brown. Leave it to cool slightly, then add the cornflour, egg yolks and liquid glucose and whisk well. Pour in the caramel mixture, whisking constantly, then cook over a low heat until the custard thickens slightly. Keep stirring with a spatula. Pass the mixture through a fine sieve, then chill and churn it in an ice-cream machine until frozen.

For salted caramel ice cream, use good salted butter or add 2 teaspoons of flaked sea salt to the custard mixture.

SERVES 12

260g caster sugar
150ml water
600ml milk
600ml double cream
300g unsalted butter
15g cornflour
9 free-range egg yolks
60g liquid glucose

Glaces aux bananes et rhum

BANANA AND RUM ICE CREAM

If the bananas are not fully ripe, leave them in a warm place or even put them in a very low oven for 3 hours.

Peel the bananas and blitz them in a food processor or blender with the sugar, rum and lemon juice. Slowly add the cream, blending until smooth. Pour the mixture into an ice-cream machine and churn until frozen.

SERVES 12

1kg very ripe bananas
    (peeled weight)
650g caster sugar
175ml good-quality dark
    rum
juice of 1 lemon
1 litre single cream

Glace aux pistaches

PISTACHIO ICE CREAM

Put the egg yolks and half the sugar into a large bowl and whisk until thick and creamy. Bring the milk and the remaining sugar to the boil, then remove from the heat, add the pistachio paste and stir to dissolve. Pour the hot milk into the yolk mixture and stir well. Pour the mixture back into the saucepan and stir over a low heat until the mixture thickens enough to coat the spoon.

Leave to cool, then strain the mixture into an ice-cream machine and churn until frozen but not too stiff. Stir in the pistachios and freeze until needed.

SERVES 8

6 free-range egg yolks
120g caster sugar
500ml full-fat milk
30g pistachio paste
30g peeled pistachios,
    roughly chopped

Glace au miel

HONEY ICE CREAM

Bring the milk to the boil in a saucepan. Meanwhile, whisk the eggs with the honey until thick and creamy, then slowly whisk in the cream. Pour the boiling milk on to the yolk mixture and whisk vigorously. Strain the mixture through a sieve and leave to cool. Chill, then churn in an ice-cream machine until frozen.

SERVES 8

500ml milk
4 free-range egg yolks
250g flower-scented clear
    honey
300ml double cream

Sorbet au chocolat amer

BITTER CHOCOLATE SORBET

Bring the water to the boil with the sugar, glucose and cocoa powder, whisking well to dissolve. Add the chopped chocolate and bring to the boil again. Leave to cool and then churn in an ice-cream machine until frozen.

SERVES 12

700ml water
240g caster sugar
80g glucose liquid
150g cocoa powder
150g extra bitter chocolate
(70% cocoa solids),
chopped

Le trou Gascon

ARMAGNAC SORBET

This sorbet can be served in the middle of a meal to refresh and cleanse the palate or as a dessert with some fresh grapes that have been peeled and steeped in Armagnac.

Pour 500ml of the water into a pan, add the sugar and glucose and bring to the boil, stirring occasionally to dissolve the sugar. Boil for 3 minutes. Add the remaining water and the wine and Armagnac to the boiling syrup, then remove from the heat, cover and leave to cool. When cold, churn in an ice-cream machine until frozen, then serve immediately.

SERVES 8

750ml water
500g granulated sugar
50g glucose
250ml dry white wine
250ml Armagnac

In France, bread is thought of as more than food;
it is a symbol of life itself and must be given proper
respect. Bread should never be placed upside down
on the table, for example – that could bring bad luck.
A French meal is not complete without bread and it's
served at every opportunity, to savour, enjoy – and to
mop up the juices on the plate. The French will even
eat bread with bread! Bakers bake throughout the day
and many people will visit their local bakery at least a
couple of times a day to buy the freshest loaves, warm
from the oven.

Pain et croissants

Fougasse

OLIVE FLATBREAD

A Mediterranean-style flatbread, fougasse is excellent served with tapenade or vegetable soups.

Dissolve the yeast in a little of the warm water in a large bowl. Add the flour, salt, the rest of the water and the olive oil, then knead until the dough is smooth and very elastic – this will take about 10 minutes. Cover the dough with a damp cloth and leave it to rise in a warm place for about an hour, or until doubled in size.

Knead the dough again briefly and add the olives. Roll it out on a floured surface to form a rough leaf shape, about 15mm thick, and place this on a baking sheet. Using a sharp knife, cut 6 or 7 slits in the dough and open them up so you can see the baking sheet.

Preheat the oven to 240°C /Fan 220°C/Gas 9. Brush the dough lightly with the beaten egg, sprinkle with coarse salt and bake for 9 minutes until golden brown. Leave to cool on a wire rack.

MAKES 1 LARGE LOAF

20g fresh yeast
350ml warm water
500g multi-grain flour, plus
   extra for rolling
1 tsp salt
4 tbsp olive oil
60g good-quality olives,
   pitted and cut in half
1 free-range egg, beaten
coarse sea salt

Pissaladière

ONION AND OLIVE TART

This variation on pizza is popular in southern France and has a puff pastry base instead of dough. It's simple to make but do allow plenty of time for the onions to cook so they are really tender and sticky.

Cut the onions in half and slice them very thinly. Heat 2 tablespoons of olive oil in a large heavy-based pan over a medium heat and add the onions, bay leaf and thyme. Season lightly with salt, generously with pepper, then cook for 35–40 minutes, stirring frequently, until the onions are very tender, sweet and light brown in colour. Leave to cool.

Roll out the pastry into a circle that's about 2–3mm thick and fold over the edges to make a raised rim. Prick the base with a fork and lightly brush the edges with the beaten egg. Refrigerate for an hour.

Preheat the oven to 240°C/Fan 220°C/Gas 9. Spread the onions thickly over the pastry base and arrange the olives and anchovies on top. Cook for about 15 minutes until the pastry is a light golden colour. Brush the pissaladière with olive oil and serve warm.

SERVES 4

6 large onions, peeled
olive oil
1 bay leaf
3–4 sprigs of thyme
200g puff pastry
1 free-range egg, beaten
30 black olives (preferably the small variety from Nice)
12 salted anchovy fillets
salt
black pepper

Pain aux ceps et l'ail confit

CEPS AND GARLIC BREAD

This wonderful bread is flavoured with dried ceps and the delicate sweetness of confit garlic – garlic cloves cooked slowly and gently in olive oil. Good served on its own or with a seasonal salad.

Cover the ceps with 150ml of the water and leave them to soak for 30 minutes. Dissolve the yeast in the rest of the water in a large bowl, then stir in the white flour with a wooden spatula. Cover and leave in a warm place to rise and double in volume. Drain the ceps (reserving the liquid) and fry them in the olive oil for 1 minute. Drain again and set aside.

In the bowl of a food mixer, put the soaking water of the ceps, the spelt and rye flours, thyme leaves, a pinch of salt and the risen first dough. Knead at a low speed with the dough hook for 10 minutes. Scrape down the dough from the edges of the bowl and knead for another 2 minutes. Cover and leave to rise for 30 minutes.

Knock the dough back, then gently work in the ceps and confit garlic cloves without breaking them up. Do this by folding the bread over on itself several times. Shape the dough into a loaf and place it on a floured baking sheet, then cover and leave to rise for 30 minutes. Preheat the oven to 220°C/Fan 200°C/Gas 7 and bake the loaf for 35–40 minutes. Cool on a wire rack.

CONFIT GARLIC

Separate the garlic cloves, peel them and blanch in boiling water. Drain and put the cloves on a piece of foil, sprinkle with sea salt and a generous amount of olive oil, then wrap up in the foil to make a loose 'bag'. Place this on a baking sheet and bake in the oven at 170°C/Fan 150°C/Gas 3½ for about 30 minutes. Shake the garlic in the foil 'bag' a few times during the cooking. Leave to cool before using.

MAKES 1 LARGE LOAF

60g dried ceps
425ml warm water
25g fresh yeast
400g strong white bread
    flour, plus extra for
    dusting
1 tbsp olive oil
100g spelt flour
100g rye flour
1 tbsp thyme leaves, picked
    from the stems
12 confit garlic cloves
salt

CONFIT GARLIC

1 garlic bulb
olive oil
sea salt

Pain à l'huile d'olive

OLIVE OIL BREAD

This simple white bread is similar to a baguette and is
great for sandwiches. It also makes good croutons, as it
crisps up well in the oven.

MAKES 1 LOAF

12g fresh yeast

275ml warm water

500g strong unbleached
   stoneground bread flour

4 tbsp olive oil

1 heaped tsp fine salt

milk, for brushing

1 pinch of coarse sea salt

Dissolve the yeast in the warm water, add the flour and knead for 15 minutes
until silky and elastic. Add the olive oil and fine salt, then knead again for 5
minutes. Cover the dough and leave it to rise for 40 minutes.

Knock back the dough and form it into a long loaf. Place this on a non-stick
baking sheet, cover and leave to rise for another 20 minutes. Preheat the
oven to 220°C/Fan 200°C/Gas 7. Lightly brush the top of the loaf with milk
and add a sprinkling of coarse sea salt, then place it in the oven and bake for
30 minutes or until cooked through. Cool on a wire rack.

Brioche

RICH SWEET BREAD

Brioche dough is enriched with eggs so is richer than croissants. It makes a delicious cake-like bread that is good served at breakfast – or any other time of day. It's excellent with savoury terrines too.

MAKES 1 LARGE LOAF
OR 30 SMALL BUNS

15g fresh yeast
500g plain flour, sifted, plus
   extra for dusting
7 free-range eggs
2 tsp salt
50g sugar
300g softened butter

Place the yeast in a food mixer bowl with a few drops of water to soften it. Add the sifted flour, 6 of the eggs, one at a time, and the salt and sugar, then slowly knead with the dough attachment. You can do this by hand but you get a better result with a machine.

After 5 minutes, the dough should be smooth and elastic. Add the softened butter and continue to knead at a slightly faster speed for 10 minutes. Make sure all the butter has been incorporated. Put the dough in a large, clean container, cover it with cling film and leave it in the fridge for 12 hours. After 4 hours, knock the dough back by punching it firmly to release the fermentation gases.

Tip the brioche dough out on to a floured surface and roll it into a loaf tin or shape it into 30 balls and place them on a baking tray. Leave in a warm, draught-free place until risen by a third. Preheat the oven to 200°C/Fan 180°C/Gas 6. Beat the remaining egg and use it to brush the surface of the brioche, then cook until golden. A loaf will take about 40 minutes to cook and small brioche rolls about 15 minutes.

Croissants

CROISSANTS

Every bakery in France displays trays of freshly baked
croissants for that quick morning mouthful with a cup
of coffee. If you've never made your own it's well worth a
try and once you get the knack of folding them correctly
it's not that hard. You can also freeze the croissants
once rolled and then whip them out of the freezer an
hour before cooking. Enjoy them warm from the oven.

Dissolve the yeast in the warm water and milk powder. Add this to the
sifted flour, sugar, salt and the 40g of melted butter. Knead well by hand
or machine for 4–5 minutes until the dough is smooth and everything is
incorporated, but do not overwork. Cover and leave the dough to rise until
doubled in size.

Roll the dough out to about A4 size. Place the 300g of room-temperature
butter in the middle and fold over the edges of the dough to enclose the
butter completely. Dust the dough with flour and gently roll it out to a
rectangle measuring about 40 x 26cm. Take both ends, fold them to the
centre and fold again to make a much smaller rectangle. Wrap in cling film
and refrigerate for an hour, then repeat the process of rolling out and folding
the dough.

Roll the dough out on a floured surface to a thickness of 1cm and cut it into 30
triangles, each with a base of 12cm. Roll each triangle towards the point, then
bring the points together to form the croissant shape. Place the croissants on
a baking tray and leave them to rise for about 20 minutes. Preheat the oven to
180°C/Fan 160°C/Gas 4.

Brush the croissants with beaten egg and bake for 15 minutes until cooked.

MAKES 30 SMALL CROISSANTS

45g fresh yeast
400g warm water
40g milk powder
800g flour, sifted, plus extra
    for dusting
80g sugar
20g salt
40g butter, melted
300g butter, at room
    temperature
1 free-range egg, beaten

Pain de mie au lait

SANDWICH BREAD LOAF

Easy to make, this bread tastes great and is very
satisfying. You can vary the recipe as you like and add
wheatgerm, bran and a little rye or wholemeal flour
instead of some of the white. A few cumin seeds mixed
through the dough are also a good addition. If you are
lactose intolerant, use water instead of the milk and oil
instead of butter, but this does make it less rich. You
will need 2 loaf tins measuring about 20 x 12cm.

MAKES 2 LOAVES

10g yeast
350ml warm milk
250g plain flour, plus extra
    for dusting
250g strong bread flour
20g golden syrup
10g sea salt
25g melted butter

Dissolve the yeast in the warm milk in a large bowl, then add all the other
ingredients. Mix thoroughly until lump free, then cover the dough and leave
for 5 minutes.

Turn the dough out on a lightly floured surface and knead it for 10 minutes
until smooth and elastic. Put the dough back in the bowl, cover and leave to
ferment and rise for at least an hour or until almost doubled in size. Knock it
back and shape it into 2 equal balls. Place these in lightly greased and floured
bread tins, cover and leave to rise again.

Preheat the oven to 220°C/Fan 200°C/Gas 7. Using a razor blade or a very
sharp knife, carefully slash the top of each loaf and immediately put them in
the oven. After 10 minutes, turn down the oven to 180°C/Fan 160°C/Gas 4
and continue to bake for 30 minutes. When cooked, tip the loaves out of the
tins and leave them to cool on a wire rack.

*En France, la cuisine est
une sérieuse forme d'art et
un sport national*

In France, cooking is a serious
art form and a national sport

JULIA CHILD

Pain au cacao

CHOCOLATE BREAD

This sweet, bitter bread is perfect served with rich
winter dishes such as braised meats or game.

Dissolve the yeast in a little of the tepid water in a large bowl. Add the rest
of the ingredients and mix until the dough comes together, adding a couple
drops more water if needed. Knead for 10 minutes until the dough is supple
and elastic, then cover and leave to rise for an hour.

Knock the dough back and shape it into a round loaf. Cover and leave to rise
again for about 45 minutes or until it has doubled in size. Preheat the oven
to 240°C/Fan 220°C/Gas 9. Dust the loaf with cocoa powder and carefully
slash the top with a razor blade or a very sharp knife. Cook for 20 minutes,
then turn the oven down to 180°C/Fan 160°/Gas 4 and cook for a further 30
minutes. Remove the bread and cool on a wire rack.

1 LOAF

15g yeast
360ml tepid water
400g white bread flour
100g extra-bitter cocoa
   powder, plus extra for
   dusting
1 tbsp brown sugar
1 tsp salt

Pain aux noix et yaourt

WALNUT AND YOGHURT BREAD

This bread is quick and easy to make and is good with
cheese or simply lashings of salted butter.

Mix all the dry ingredients together in a bowl. Put all the wet ingredients in
a separate bowl and whisk, then combine the wet with the dry and mix well
for 3–4 minutes. The dough should be fairly wet. Preheat the oven to 220°C/
Fan 200°C/Gas 7.

Put the dough into a 1kg non-stick loaf tin. Place it in the oven and
immediately turn the heat down to 200°C/180°C/Gas 6 and bake the loaf
for an hour or until golden and fully cooked. Take the loaf out of the tin and
leave to cool on a wire rack.

1 LOAF

360g plain flour
140g wholemeal flour
1 tbsp bicarbonate of soda
1 tbsp baking powder
100g chopped walnuts
½ tbsp honey
200g plain yoghurt
1 tbsp vegetable oil

Pizza aux artichauts

ARTICHOKE PIZZA

This is not a classic Italian recipe but one that I used to make when working as an apprentice in a pastry shop. The base is more like a rich brioche than pizza dough.

Put the yeast in a bowl and pour on the water and milk. Mix well, then add the flour, salt, sugar, egg and melted butter. Knead for 4–5 minutes until the dough is elastic, shiny and smooth, then cover the bowl and refrigerate for at least 3 hours.

Trim the artichokes and rub them with a cut lemon to prevent them from going brown. Thinly slice the onions and garlic. Heat a little olive oil in a pan and sear the sliced artichokes for 2–3 minutes, then add the onions and garlic. Once they have taken on a little colour, season with salt and pepper and take the pan off the heat.

Take the dough out of the fridge and divide it into 8 balls. Place these on a floured surface, roll them out to about 5mm thick and put them on a non-stick baking sheet. Divide the topping evenly over the bases, then leave for 20 minutes to rise. Preheat the oven to 240°C/Fan 220°C/Gas 9. Just before placing the pizzas in the oven, grate the cheese on top and drizzle with a little olive oil. Bake for about 10 minutes, then remove and serve.

SERVES 8

DOUGH

15g yeast
180ml tepid water
50ml milk
500g bread flour, plus
    extra for dusting
10g salt
1 tsp sugar
1 free-range egg, beaten
75g melted butter

TOPPING

8–12 small globe artichokes
    (poivrade)
1 lemon
2 large onions, peeled
3 garlic cloves, peeled
olive oil
2 very dry hard goat cheeses
    (crottin or Pélardon)
salt
black pepper

Pain Tunisien

SESAME-FLAVOURED BREAD

This bread is perfect with all North African dishes, but give me some warm from the oven with just a few olives or dates or a hunk of good cheese and I'm happy.

Dissolve the yeast in the water, then add the semolina, flour, salt and oil. Mix to form a dough, then knead for 10 minutes until smooth and elastic. Cover and leave to rise in a warm place for about an hour or until it has doubled in size.

Knock the dough back, place it on a floured surface and shape it into 2 balls. Using a rolling pin, roll these out into circles of about 20cm across and 3cm thick. Place them on a baking sheet, cover and leave to double in size again. Preheat the oven to 220°C/Fan 200°C/Gas 7. Gently brush the dough with beaten egg and sprinkle with sesame seeds, then bake for 30 minutes.

2 SMALL LOAVES

15g yeast
150ml tepid water
250g fine semolina (finest possible)
250g white bread flour, plus extra for dusting
1 tbsp salt
100ml olive oil
1 free-range egg, beaten
2 tbsp sesame seeds

Stocks are the cornerstones of great cooking. You can buy good fresh stocks now, of course, but there's nothing like making your own for the best results. They're easy to prepare and allow you to make use of all the bones and trimmings from your meat and fish so there's no waste! I'm a big fan of sauces too, which can provide the finishing touch to a dish. Every keen cook should try to learn the basics, like a good meat jus and a classic vinaigrette. You'll also find some other little extras in this chapter, which can help to make your cooking something special.

Bouillons
et sauces

Bouillon de légumes

VEGETABLE STOCK

Peel or trim and roughly chop all the vegetables and put them in a large saucepan with the cold water. Add the herbs and bring the water to the boil. Simmer for about 35 minutes, then strain the stock before using. It can be kept in the fridge for up to 5 days.

MAKES 2 LITRES

1 carrot

2 shallots

1 small onion

2 celery sticks

1 leek (green top part only)

2.5 litres water

1 bay leaf

1 bunch of thyme

a handful of parsley stalks

Bouillon de volaille

CHICKEN STOCK

Place the bones, or wing tips, and the calf's foot in a large pan, cover with the water and bring to the boil. Skim off the scum and fat that comes to the surface. Turn the heat down, add the remaining ingredients and simmer for $1\frac{1}{2}$ hours, skimming occasionally.

Pass the stock through a fine sieve and leave to cool. It can be kept in the fridge for up to 5 days, or it can be frozen.

MAKES ABOUT 4 LITRES

2kg chicken bones or wing tips

1 calf's foot, split

5 litres water

1 onion, peeled and roughly chopped

1 small leek, roughly chopped

2 celery sticks, roughly chopped

2 sprigs of thyme

6 parsley stalks

Bouillon de volaille brun

BROWN CHICKEN STOCK

A brown chicken stock is used for soups, sauces and other dishes that require a little extra depth and colour, such as a consommé or a stew.

Preheat the oven to 220°C/Fan 200°C/Gas 7. Put the bones, or wing tips, and the calf's foot in a roasting pan, drizzle them with olive oil and roast until brown. Transfer the bones to a deep saucepan, cover with 5 litres of the cold water and bring to a gentle simmer.

Meanwhile, place the roasting pan on the hob, add the vegetables and garlic, then fry until golden. Add the tomato paste, thyme and the remaining litre of water, then bring to the boil, stirring well to scrape up any caramelised bits sticking to the bottom of the pan. Once boiling, pour all the contents into the saucepan with the bones and continue to simmer for 2 hours, skimming when necessary. Pass the stock through a fine sieve and chill. The stock can be kept in the fridge for 5 days or it can be frozen.

MAKES ABOUT 5 LITRES

2kg chicken bones or wing tips
1 calf's foot, split
olive oil
6 litres cold water
1 onion, peeled and roughly chopped
1 carrot, peeled and roughly chopped
1 celery stick, roughly chopped
5 garlic cloves, peeled and roughly chopped
1 tbsp tomato paste
2 sprigs of thyme

Bouillon de canard

DUCK STOCK

Preheat the oven to 220°C/Fan 200°C/Gas 7. Put the bones and calf's foot in a roasting pan with a little oil and roast until well browned. Transfer them to a deep saucepan and cover with about 500ml of the water.

Put the onion, carrot and celery in the roasting pan and brown on the hob, then add to the saucepan with the bones. Place the roasting pan over a high heat and add the remaining 4 litres of cold water. Bring to the boil, scraping the bottom of the pan with a wooden spatula to loosen any caramelised bits, then pour the liquid into the saucepan with the bones.

Simmer for 2 hours, occasionally skimming off the fat and scum from the surface, then pass the stock through a sieve and chill. The stock can be kept in the fridge for up to 7 days, or it can be frozen.

MAKES ABOUT 3 LITRES

2kg duck bones

½ calf's foot, split

olive oil

4.5 litres water

1 onion, peeled and roughly chopped

1 carrot, peeled and roughly chopped

2 celery sticks, roughly chopped

Bouillon de veau

VEAL STOCK

Preheat the oven to 220°C/Fan 200°C/Gas 7. Put the bones and calf's foot in a roasting pan with a little oil and roast them in the oven, turning occasionally until brown all over. Transfer them to a large saucepan.

Put the onion, carrots and celery into the roasting pan and roast them in the oven until golden, turning frequently with a wooden spatula. Pour off any excess fat and put the vegetables into the saucepan with the bones. Place the roasting pan over a high heat and add 500ml of the water. Bring to the boil, scraping the bottom of the pan to loosen any caramelised bits, then pour everything into the saucepan with the bones.

Add the remaining ingredients and the rest of the water and bring to the boil. Skim off the scum and fat, then turn down the heat and simmer gently for 3½ hours, skimming occasionally. Pass the stock through a fine sieve and leave to cool. The stock can be kept in the fridge for up to 7 days, or it can be frozen.

MAKES ABOUT 3.5 LITRES

1.5kg veal knuckle bones, chopped

1 calf's foot, split

olive oil

1 large onion, peeled and roughly chopped

2 large carrots, peeled and roughly chopped

1 celery stick, roughly chopped

5 litres water

2 garlic cloves, peeled

2 sprigs of thyme

½ tbsp tomato purée

Bouillon de boeuf

BEEF STOCK

Preheat the oven to 220°C/Fan 200°C/Gas 7. Put the bones and trotters in a roasting pan with a little oil and roast them in the oven, turning occasionally, until brown all over. Transfer them to a large saucepan and pour in enough water to cover by 15cm.

Pour off some of the fat from the roasting pan, add the onions, carrot and celery, then roast until golden. Add the vegetables and all the other ingredients to the bones. Put the roasting pan over a high heat. Pour in 500ml of water to deglaze the pan, scraping the bottom to loosen the caramelised bits, then pour into the pan with the bones. Bring to the boil, skim off the scum, then lower the heat and simmer for 2½ hours, skimming frequently. Strain and chill. The stock can be kept in the fridge for up to 7 days, or it can be frozen.

MAKES ABOUT 5 LITRES

3kg beef bones, chopped

3 pigs' trotters, split

olive oil

2 onions, peeled and
  roughly chopped

1 carrot, peeled and roughly
  chopped

2 celery sticks, roughly
  chopped

2 bay leaves

1 sprig of thyme

1 bunch of parsley stalks

2 tsp peppercorns

3 beefsteak tomatoes,
  chopped

1 leek top (green top
  part only)

Court bouillon

CLEAR POACHING STOCK

This is a perfect stock for poaching fish and for cooking lobsters. It can then be used as the basis of a fish stock or sauce.

Slice the vegetables into thin 3mm rounds. Bring the water, wine and vinegar to the boil, add all the vegetables, the bouquet garni, salt and the peppercorns tied in a little muslin bag. Simmer for 15 minutes until the vegetables are cooked but still a little crunchy. Strain and chill. This can be kept in the fridge for 3–4 days.

MAKES ABOUT 3.5 LITRES

2 carrots, peeled

white part of 1 leek

1 celery stick

½ fennel bulb

4 shallots, peeled

2 small white onions, peeled

1.5 litres water

1 bottle of dry white wine

2 tbsp white wine vinegar

1 bouquet garni

25g coarse sea salt

1 tbsp cracked black or
   white peppercorns

Bouillon de poisson

FISH STOCK

Remove any gills from the fish heads, then soak the heads and bones in cold water for 3–4 hours. Remove them from the water and chop roughly. Melt the butter in a deep saucepan and sweat the onion and celery over a low heat until softened. Add the fish bones and heads and cook for 2–3 minutes, stirring frequently.

Pour in the wine, turn up the heat and reduce by half. Add the water and herbs and bring to the boil, skimming frequently. Lower the heat and simmer, uncovered, for 25 minutes. Strain through a muslin-lined sieve and leave to cool. This can be kept in the fridge for 2–3 days or it can be frozen.

MAKES ABOUT 2 LITRES

1kg bones and heads from
   white fish (sole, whiting,
   turbot)

4 tbsp unsalted butter

1 small onion, peeled and
   roughly chopped

1 celery stick, roughly
   chopped

60g dry white wine

2 litres water

6 parsley stalks

1 bay leaf

Bouillon de homard

LOBSTER STOCK

I've specified lobster heads because the claws and body have little flavour, although you can add them if you have room in the pan. Add langoustine and prawn heads too if you have them.

Crush the lobster heads with a mallet or a rolling pin until they are well broken up. Heat the olive oil in a large saucepan and sweat the onion, carrot and celery. When the vegetables are lightly browned, add the herbs and lobster heads, stirring to prevent them from sticking to the pan. After about 5 minutes, stir in the tomatoes, tomato purée and cayenne pepper. Pour in the brandy and stir well for a couple of minutes, then add the wine and boil for at least 3 minutes.

Add the stocks and bring to the boil, then season lightly with sea salt. Simmer for 40 minutes, stirring occasionally and skimming off any scum that appears on the surface.

Drain the stock through a colander set over a large bowl, pressing the lobster heads well to extract all the juices and flavour. Then pass this liquid through a fine sieve into a clean saucepan, bring it to the boil and skim. The stock can be kept in the fridge for 2–3 days or it can be frozen.

MAKES ABOUT 3 LITRES

3kg lobster heads
2 tbsp olive oil
1 large onion, peeled and
    chopped
1 carrot, peeled and
    chopped
2 celery sticks, chopped
4 parsley stalks
1 sprig of thyme
1 bay leaf
2 large tomatoes
2 tbsp tomato purée
½ tsp cayenne pepper
1 tbsp brandy
300ml dry white wine
2 litres fish stock
1 litre veal stock
    (see page 322)
sea salt

Dans la cuisine, les sauces sont
comme les premiers rudiments
de grammaire — le fondement de
toutes les langues

Sauces in cookery are like the first rudiments of
grammar — the foundation of all languages
ALEXIS SOYER

Jus de volaille

CHICKEN JUS

While a stock is the foundation of a sauce, a jus has a more intense flavour and more body. It needs only a little butter or other finishing touch to make it into a sauce.

Preheat the oven to 220°C/Fan 200°C/Gas 7. Put the bones in a roasting pan and roast them in the oven, turning occasionally, until brown all over. Transfer the bones to a deep pan.

Brown the shallots in the roasting pan, stirring frequently. Add the wine and stir to loosen all the residue. Boil to reduce by half, then pour into the pan with the bones. Add the stock and bring to the boil. Simmer for 45 minutes, skimming occasionally, then strain.

MAKES ABOUT 2 LITRES

1kg chicken bones, chopped
   small
3 shallots, chopped
100ml dry white wine
2.5 litres chicken stock
   (see page 320)

Jus de boeuf

BEEF JUS

Preheat the oven to 220°C/Fan 200°C/Gas 7. Put the bones or trimmings in a roasting pan and roast them in the oven, turning occasionally, until brown all over. Transfer them to a deep saucepan.

Brown the onion in the roasting pan, stirring frequently. Add the wine and stir to loosen all the caramelised bits on the bottom of the pan. Boil to reduce by half, then pour into the pan with the bones. Add the thyme, garlic and veal stock and bring to the boil. Simmer for 45 minutes, skimming occasionally, then strain.

MAKES ABOUT 2 LITRES

1kg beef bones or lean
   trimmings, chopped
   small
1 onion, peeled and sliced
200ml dry white wine
2 sprigs of thyme
2 garlic cloves
2.5 litres veal stock
   (see page 322)

Jus de veau

VEAL JUS

Preheat the oven to 220°C/Fan 200°C/Gas 7. Put the bones in a roasting pan and roast them in the oven, turning occasionally, until brown all over. Transfer the bones to a deep saucepan.

Brown the shallots in the roasting pan, stirring frequently. Add the wine and stir to loosen all the residue. Boil to reduce by half, then pour into the saucepan with the bones. Add the stock and bring to the boil. Simmer for 45 minutes, skimming occasionally, then strain.

MAKES ABOUT 2 LITRES

1kg veal bones, chopped
   small
3 shallots, chopped
200ml dry white wine
2.5 litres veal stock
   (see page 322)

Jus de gibier

GAME JUS

Preheat the oven to 220°C/Fan 200°C/Gas 7. Put the bones in a roasting pan and roast them in the oven, turning occasionally, until brown all over. Transfer the bones to a deep saucepan.

Brown the shallots in the roasting pan, stirring frequently. Add the Madeira and juniper berries and stir to loosen all the residue. Boil to reduce by half, then pour into the saucepan with the bones. Add the stock and bring to the boil. Simmer for 45 minutes, skimming occasionally, then strain.

MAKES ABOUT 2 LITRES

1kg game bird bones,
   chopped small
3 shallots, chopped
200ml Madeira wine
5 juniper berries, crushed
2.5 litres chicken stock
   (see page 320)

Jus d'agneau

LAMB JUS

Preheat the oven to 220°C/Fan 200°C/Gas 7. Put the bones in a roasting pan and roast them in the oven, turning occasionally, until brown all over. Transfer the bones to a deep saucepan.

Brown the onion in the roasting pan, stirring frequently. Add the wine and stir to loosen all the caramelised bits on the bottom of the pan. Boil to reduce by half, then pour into the saucepan with the bones. Add the thyme, garlic and veal stock and bring to the boil. Simmer for 45 minutes, skimming occasionally, then strain.

MAKES ABOUT 2 LITRES

1kg lamb bones, chopped
   small
1 onion, sliced
250ml dry white wine
2 sprigs of thyme
2 garlic cloves
2.5 litres veal stock

Sauce Hollandaise

HOLLANDAISE SAUCE

Boil the vinegar in a small pan with the peppercorns and salt, then take the pan off the heat. Add the water and egg yolks, transfer the mixture to a double boiler (not too hot) or a bowl set over a pan of simmering water and whisk for about 8–10 minutes until the egg yolks are light and creamy. Don't let the mixture get too hot or the egg yolks will scramble.

Take the mixture off the heat and pour in the clarified butter, whisking continuously. Pass the sauce through a fine sieve, and add a little lemon juice to taste.

CLARIFIED BUTTER

Melt the butter in a small pan over a low heat until it foams. Spoon off the foam and let the butter settle. Remove the clarified butter with a ladle, discarding the whitish residue in the base of the pan.

MAKES 150ML

2 tsp white wine vinegar

1 tsp cracked white peppercorns

pinch of salt

2 tbsp water

4 free-range egg yolks

225g unsalted butter, clarified

lemon juice, to taste

Sauce Béarnaise

BÉARNAISE SAUCE

Put the shallots in a pan with the tarragon, vinegar, peppercorns and the tablespoon of water and boil to reduce by half. Remove from the heat and leave to cool. When cold, add the egg yolks and whisk the mixture in a double boiler – or in a bowl set over a pan of simmering water – for 8–10 minutes until the yolks are light and creamy. Don't let the mixture get too hot, or the eggs will scramble.

Take the mixture off the heat and gently pour in the clarified butter, whisking constantly. Season with a little salt and add the fresh snipped chervil before serving.

SAUCE PALOISE
Use fresh mint instead of tarragon and chervil. Delicious with grilled lamb.

SAUCE CHORON
Peel, deseed and chop 5 ripe plum tomatoes and sweat them in a little butter to remove the excess moisture. Add to the finished Béarnaise sauce.

MAKES 175ML

2 shallots, peeled and finely chopped

3 tbsp snipped fresh tarragon

3 tbsp white wine vinegar or tarragon vinegar

1 tsp crushed white peppercorns

1 tbsp water

4 free-range egg yolks

250g unsalted butter, clarified (see opposite)

2 tbsp snipped fresh chervil

salt

Beurre blanc

BUTTER SAUCE

Put the wine, vinegar and shallots in a thick-based saucepan. Bring to the boil and continue to cook until the liquid is reduced by half. Add the cream and boil for 1 minute, then lower the heat and gradually whisk in the cubes of cold butter.

I like to keep the shallots in the sauce, but if you prefer a smoother finish, pass the sauce through a fine sieve. Season with salt and pepper to taste.

MAKES ABOUT 300ML

100ml dry white wine

1 tbsp white wine vinegar

2 shallots, peeled and finely chopped

50ml double cream

200g cold unsalted butter, cubed

salt

black pepper

Mayonnaise

Put the egg yolks, mustard, salt and vinegar in a round-bottomed bowl and mix with a balloon whisk until smooth. Gradually pour in all the oil in a steady stream, whisking continuously until the mixture is rich and creamy.

This can be kept in a covered container in the fridge for up to a week.

MAKES ABOUT 600ML

2 free-range egg yolks

1 tbsp Dijon mustard

1 tsp fine salt

½ tbsp white wine vinegar

500ml vegetable oil

50ml extra virgin olive oil

Mayonnaise aux herbes

HERB MAYONNAISE

Put all the ingredients except the oil in a blender and blitz. With the blender on full speed, slowly pour in the oil.

MAKES ABOUT 260ML

2 free-range egg yolks
½ tbsp Dijon mustard
1 tbsp tarragon vinegar
6 tbsp chopped fresh herbs
    (chives, tarragon, flatleaf
    parsley, dill)
1 tsp salt
black pepper
260ml vegetable oil

Aïoli

GARLIC MAYONNAISE

Slice the garlic lengthways, removing any green shoots, then put the garlic in a blender with the egg yolks, mustard, vinegar, salt and cayenne pepper, and blend at full speed.

Gradually trickle in the olive oil while the blender is running. After half of the oil has been incorporated, stop and scrape down the sides of the blender with a spatula.

Continue to trickle in the oil, scraping the sides of the blender once or twice more, and adding 1–2 tablespoons of cold water with the last of the oil to thin the consistency slightly, until you have a smooth garlic mayonnaise.

MAKES ABOUT 275ML

5 garlic cloves, peeled
2 free-range egg yolks
1 tsp Dijon mustard
2 tsp white wine vinegar
pinch of salt
pinch of cayenne pepper
275ml light olive oil
1–2 tbsp cold water

Sauce vin rouge

RED WINE SAUCE

Fry the beef trimmings in a pan with a little olive oil until crisp. Drain off the fat, add the wine and port and reduce by half, occasionally skimming off the fat and scum that come to the surface.

Heat a little olive oil in another pan and cook the onion, shallots and bacon until well browned. Add the peppercorns and then pour in the reduced wine, followed by the stock. Bring to the boil and skim, then turn down the heat and simmer for 35 minutes. Pass the sauce through a fine sieve.

To serve with steaks, bring the sauce to the boil and reduce until slightly thickened. Take the pan off the heat and whisk in a little cold butter, cut into small cubes.

MAKES 1.5 LITRES

120g beef trimmings
  (bone or sinew)
olive oil
1 bottle of full-bodied red
  wine (Syrah or Shiraz)
100ml port
1 onion, peeled and sliced
2 shallots, peeled and sliced
80g smoked bacon, chopped
1 tsp cracked white and black
  peppercorns
2 litres veal stock
  (see page 322)

Sauce à l'estragon

TARRAGON SAUCE

Melt a tablespoon of the butter in a pan and sweat the shallots over a low heat until softened but not coloured. When the shallots are soft, deglaze the pan with the tarragon vinegar and wine, then reduce the liquid until the pan is nearly dry.

Pour in the stock and reduce until syrupy. Add the cream and boil for 2 minutes, then whisk in the remaining butter, season to taste and add the tarragon leaves just before serving with chicken or poached fish. Do not strain this sauce, as the texture of the shallots adds another dimension.

MAKES 250ML

2 tbsp unsalted butter
2 shallots, peeled and finely
  chopped
2 tbsp tarragon vinegar
100ml dry white wine
400ml chicken stock
  (see page 320)
100ml double cream
5 tbsp tarragon leaves,
  chopped
salt
white pepper

Vinaigrette aux herbes

HERB DRESSING

Put the egg yolks in a blender with the mustard, vinegar, salt and pepper. Blend at high speed, slowly adding the olive and vegetable oils, a little at a time. After a third of the oil has been incorporated, add the herbs. Continue to blend, adding the oils a little at a time. The vinaigrette should have the consistency of pouring cream. If the mixture becomes too thick, add a few drops of cold water to the blender.

If you want to remove the herbs, pass the vinaigrette through a fine sieve. This can be kept in the fridge for up to 2 weeks.

MAKES ABOUT 500ML

2 free-range egg yolks
1 tsp Dijon mustard
1½ tbsp tarragon vinegar
150ml extra virgin olive oil
300ml vegetable oil
1 tbsp each of chives, flatleaf parsley and tarragon, chopped
salt
black pepper

Vinaigrette à la tomate

TOMATO DRESSING

Make a tomato 'fondue' – peel, deseed and chop 4 ripe tomatoes and cook them in a little olive oil until the mixture is thick and dry.

Make the vinaigrette as above, but replace the herbs with 1 heaped teaspoon of tomato purée and 1 heaped tablespoon of tomato 'fondue'. Season with a few drops of Tabasco sauce instead of pepper.

MAKES ABOUT 500ML

4 ripe tomatoes
150ml extra virgin olive oil, plus extra for cooking the tomatoes
2 free-range egg yolks
1 tsp Dijon mustard
1½ tbsp tarragon vinegar
1 heaped tsp tomato purée
300ml vegetable oil
Tabasco sauce

Gelée au Madère

MADEIRA JELLY

This recipe makes enough Madeira jelly for the ham mousse on page 58. It is also good served with cold meat, especially cured meats and game.

Put the gelatine leaves in a bowl of cold water to soften. Pour the wine into a small pan and bring to boiling point. Immediately take the pan off the heat and whisk in the seasoning and softened gelatine – squeeze out any excess water from the gelatine first. Pass the mixture through a fine sieve, leave to cool, then chill in the fridge until set.

8 gelatine leaves
750ml Madeira wine
2 tsp salt
1 tsp cracked black pepper

Coulis de tomates

TOMATO PURÉE

Heat the olive oil in a pan and sweat the shallots and garlic until soft but not coloured. Add the tomato paste and cook for another 3 minutes, then add the sugar, chopped tomatoes, bouquet garni, water and seasoning. Bring to a simmer, cover with a piece of greaseproof paper and cook for 20 minutes. Tip everything into a food processor and blend until smooth. Lovely served with spinach soufflés (see page 74).

Any leftover coulis can be kept in the fridge in an airtight container for up to a week and used on pizzas and pasta.

2 tbsp olive oil
2 shallots, peeled and finely chopped
3 garlic cloves, peeled and finely chopped
1 tbsp tomato paste
1 tbsp sugar
800g tomatoes, peeled, deseeded and chopped
1 bouquet garni see page 342)
2 tbsp water
salt
black pepper

Chutney de tomates vertes et potiron

GREEN TOMATO AND MARROW CHUTNEY

Wipe the marrow clean, then grate it coarsely. Discard the seeds. Chop the tomatoes and put them with the grated marrow in a colander. Sprinkle with a very generous amount of sea salt and leave to drain overnight.

Next day, put all the other ingredients in a large pan and bring them to the boil, then gently press the tomato and marrow pulp in a colander to remove as much moisture as possible before adding them to the pan. Simmer for 30–40 minutes until sticky and fragrant.

Pour the chutney into sterilised glass jars and leave them in a cool place to mature for a week before using. This is good with cooked meats or to serve with cheese.

MAKES 3 JARS

550g marrow (peeled weight)
550g green tomatoes, peeled and deseeded
190g onions, thinly sliced
1 tsp ground black pepper
25g grated fresh root ginger
1 tsp crushed coriander seeds
¼ tsp ground cloves
1 tbsp tomato paste
1 tsp Madras curry powder
125g sultanas
425g demerara sugar
550ml white wine vinegar
sea salt

Chutney de tomates aux épices

SPICY TOMATO CHUTNEY

Blanch and skin the tomatoes, then cut them in half, remove the seeds and chop them roughly. Put the chopped tomatoes in a pan with the ginger, chilli, salt, tomato paste and finely chopped garlic. Simmer over a low heat until pulpy.

Add the vinegar, sugar and raisins and simmer until the mixture thickens. Stir occasionally to prevent it sticking to the bottom of the pan. Pour the chutney into sterilised glass jars, leave to cool and store in the fridge.

MAKES 2 JARS

600g ripe red tomatoes
½ tsp ground ginger
1 tsp chilli powder
2 tsp salt
2 tsp tomato paste
3 garlic cloves, peeled and finely chopped
125ml malt vinegar
120g light muscovado sugar
50g raisins

Chips de salsifis

SALSIFY CRISPS

Peel the salsify and slice lengthways on a mandolin, making the slices as thin as possible. Heat the oil to 180°C in a large pan or a deep-fat fryer. Add the slices of salsify, a few at a time, and deep-fry until crisp. Drain them on kitchen paper to absorb any excess fat, then serve.

This method can be used to make chips from any root vegetables.

1 salsify
oil, for deep-frying

Chips de pommes

APPLE CRISPS

Preheat the oven to 140°C/Fan 120°C/Gas 1. Peel the apple and slice it as thinly as possible – if you use a Granny Smith apple you can leave the skin on. Place the slices in a single layer on a non-stick baking sheet and sprinkle lightly with icing sugar. Place them in the oven for 20 minutes or until the apple slices have completely dried out.

Place the warm apple slices on a cold, dry, flat surface. As soon as they are completely cold and set, put them in an airtight container so they stay crisp.

1 apple
1 tbsp icing sugar

Croûtons à l'ail

GARLIC CROUTONS

Thinly slice the baguette. Heat the olive oil in a wide frying pan over a
medium heat, add the garlic cloves and cook until they release their aroma.
Add the sliced baguette, in batches, and fry gently until golden brown. Drain
the croutons on kitchen paper and season with salt and piment d'Espelette.

For small fried croutons, cut some white bread into 5mm cubes or tear it
into pieces for a more rustic garnish. Heat enough vegetable oil in a pan
to shallow fry the bread. When the oil is hot and smoking, add the bread
with a couple of bruised garlic cloves and a sprig of thyme. Cook until
golden, then drain and season lightly with salt. In England, these little
croutons are also known as sippets.

MAKES ENOUGH FOR 10

1 day-old baguette
1 tbsp olive oil
2 garlic cloves, bruised
ground piment d'Espelette
salt

Pâtes à base d'algues

SEAWEED PASTA

Blitz the seaweed with the flour in a food processor to break it down, then
add the whole eggs and egg yolks and process again until the mixture comes
together in a ball. Tip the mixture out and knead the dough until it is smooth
and elastic, then leave it to rest for 20 minutes. Roll the dough out and cut it
into strips of the desired size. Cook in salted boiling water.

If you want to make this pasta in advance, roll it out, cut into ribbons and
lay on a surface dusted with semolina. Leave it to dry until needed. Seaweed
pasta is good with all seafood.

SERVES 10 AS A GARNISH
OR 4 AS MAIN COURSE

60g salted kombu seaweed
  (rinsed and dried)
500g flour
3 free-range eggs
5 free-range egg yolks

Crème Chantilly

CHANTILLY CREAM

Whisk the cream with the sugar and vanilla extract, if using, until it forms soft peaks. Serve with pastries, tarts and other desserts.

If you like, use seeds scraped from a vanilla pod instead of vanilla extract.

180ml whipping cream, chilled
30g icing sugar
1 tsp vanilla extract (optional)

Crème pâtissière

CONFECTIONERS' CUSTARD

This is great for filling choux buns, éclairs or the base of a fruit tart. If you like, you can add a little Chantilly cream to the mixture and flavour it with a liqueur or some vanilla.

Whisk the yolks with the sugar until pale and creamy, then lightly whisk in the flour. Bring the milk to the boil and pour it into the yolk mixture. Stir to mix, then tip the mixture back into the saucepan and bring to the boil, stirring continuously. Boil for about 2 minutes, continuing to stir, then remove from the heat and transfer to a bowl.

MAKES ENOUGH FOR 20 CHOUX BUNS

3 free-range egg yolks
60g caster sugar
40g plain flour, sifted
250ml milk

Tuiles au miel

HONEY TUILES

These are lovely served with ice cream or for decorating desserts such as panna cotta.

Put the butter, sugar and honey in a saucepan over a low heat until they have melted together. Tip the mixture into a bowl and leave to cool slightly, then whisk in the flour and egg whites. Chill in the fridge for at least an hour.

Preheat the oven to 180°C/Fan 160°C/Gas 4. Spread the mixture very thinly on a non-stick baking sheet and bake until pale brown – this should take about 8–10 minutes. Cut into circles while still warm and leave them to cool on a sheet of greaseproof paper.

MAKES ABOUT 30

150g unsalted butter
200g light brown sugar
150g flower-scented clear
    honey
200g plain flour
5 free-range egg whites

Coulis de mûres

BLACKBERRY PURÉE

A berry coulis makes a ideal partner for ice cream or fruit desserts, such as the pear charlotte on page 283, and is very easy to make. The honey adds depth of flavour and consistency to the purée.

Blitz the blackberries with the sugar and honey in a food processor. The quantity of sugar needed depends on the ripeness of the fruit, so add a little and taste, before adding the full amount.

300g blackberries
60–80g icing sugar
1 tbsp clear honey

Chef's notes

ARTICHOKE

To prepare an artichoke heart, take the artichoke and snap off the stem. Remove the outer leaves until you reach the soft yellow leaves. Cut off the top part of the artichoke where you see the slight indentation in these leaves, then trim off a little more to reveal the fibrous choke. Scoop out the choke with a teaspoon. Trim any dark leaves off the base of the artichoke, rub the cut surfaces with a cut lemon and leave it in a bowl of water and lemon juice while you prepare the rest.

BLANCH

To blanch vegetables, plunge them into a pan of salted boiling water for a brief period, then drain and plunge into iced water. This stops the cooking process and retains the fresh colours of the vegetables.

BOUQUET GARNI

A bouquet garni is a bundle of herbs for adding to soups, casseroles and other dishes. I vary contents to match the dish, but the classic version contains parsley stalks, bay leaf, thyme, celery and leek, all tied with string, or a piece of leek, to keep them together while cooking.

BRAISE

To cook food, usually meat, slowly with some liquid in a covered pan.

CONFIT

The word confit comes from the French verb *confire*, which means to preserve. A confit is usually prepared by cooking meat such as duck, goose or pork in its own fat and storing it in fat. You can buy confit duck and other preparations or make them yourself. Confit garlic and confit potatoes can be cooked in olive oil.

DEGLAZE

To deglaze a pan means to add stock, wine or other liquid to a hot frying pan or roasting tin in which food has been cooked, and then stir to loosen any sticky bits from the pan. This helps to maximise the flavour of the sauce or gravy.

FLAMBÉ

The process of adding alcohol to a dish and setting it alight to burn off the alcohol content.

JULIENNE

This is a term used in French cookery to describe the cutting of thin strips of vegetables such as carrots. Trim the carrot top and bottom. Cut a slice off one side to make a flat surface and place the carrot down on that surface. Cut another flat surface on one side, then cut the carrot into neat fine slices. Arrange these in a pile and cut them into thin strips, like matchsticks.

LOBSTER

A lobster can be killed by plunging a sharp knife through the head between the eyes. If you prefer a gentler method, put the lobster in the freezer for about 15 minutes. Don't leave it for too long or the texture of the meat will be spoiled.

NEW SEASON GARLIC

This is the fresh garlic, sometimes known as green or 'wet' garlic, available in spring. It has a milder, more gentle flavour than older bulbs.

PIMENT D'ESPELETTE

This mild, smoky chilli pepper comes only from the village of Espelette in the Basque area of France. The chillies are dried and used whole or flaked, or ground into a powder. In 2000, it was classified as AOC (Appellation d'Origine Contrôlée), meaning that the name is protected and the chillies can be grown only in this area. It is available from specialist grocers and internet sites. You can use regular chilli powder instead but some kinds may be a little hotter than the Espelette variety so add with care.

POACH

To cook food such as fish, eggs or meat very gently in simmering liquid.

REDUCE

To reduce liquid such as stock or sauce, boil or simmer in an open pan so the liquid evaporates by the required amount, intensifying the flavour.

SUPRÊME

This is a French term for a breast of chicken or other poultry. The breast is boned but may have the wing attached.

TRUFFLE

A truffle is a kind of fungus, which grows around the roots of certain trees. They are expensive but have the most wonderful flavour. There are many different types, but my favourite is the black winter truffle (*Tuber melanosporum*). Black truffles can be cooked but are often eaten raw – just shave thin slices over a dish.

TURNING VEGETABLES

Turning root vegetables such as carrots and turnips makes for a neat, elegant presentation and ensures that they are the same size and so cook evenly. Peel the vegetables and cut them into chunks of about 5cm long. Carefully pare the sides of each piece to make a barrel shape that slightly tapers at each end.

VENTRÈCHE

This meat comes from fatty pork belly and may be smoked or salted. If you can't get ventrèche, pancetta or streaky bacon are good substitutes.

VERJUS

This is a sour juice from unripe grapes and is not fermented. You can find verjus in good delis but if none is available, you can use light white wine instead.

Index

To Gisele and Emily – food tastes better when I am with you

Thank you all

The making of this book would not have been possible without the professionalism of chef Francesco Dibenedetto, who worked with me and prepared the food for the photographs. I would also like to thank Noemi Guy for her skill at reading my scribbled lines on sauce-stained scrap paper; Cristian Barnett for capturing the taste of the food so perfectly on film; Miranda Harvey for her skilful eye, tips on how to relax a salad and making carrots disappear; Holly Clifton-Brown for the gorgeous illustrations; Polly Webb-Wilson for the beautiful choice of plates and her navigational skills; Jinny Johnson for being as passionate about good food as I am and for making *The French Kitchen* delicious to read; Amanda Harris and Lucie Stericker at Weidenfeld & Nicolson for directing operations with such care and good humour; Gérard – my brother in law – for shooting straight and filling the freezer with game; and my neighbour Annie for the 'mucky eggs'.

First published in Great Britain in 2013
by Weidenfeld & Nicolson, an imprint of
Orion Publishing Group Ltd
Orion House, 5 Upper St Martin's Lane,
London WC2H 9EA
an Hachette UK company
10 9 8 7 6 5 4 3 2 1

Text copyright © Michel Roux Jr
Design and layout © Weidenfeld & Nicolson 2013

A CIP catalogue record for this book is available
from the British Library.

ISBN: 978 0 297 867234

Photographer: Cristian Barnett
Illustrator: Holly Clifton-Brown
Designer and art director: Miranda Harvey
Editor: Jinny Johnson
Stylist: Polly Webb-Wilson
Proofreader: Elise See Tai
Indexer: Vicki Robinson

Printed and bound in Italy

The Orion Publishing Group's policy is to
use papers that are natural, renewable and
recyclable products and made from wood
grown in sustainable forests. The logging
and manufacturing processes are expected
to conform to the environmental regulations
of the country of origin.

www.orionbooks.co.uk